Using
Metacognitive
Assessments
to Create
Individualized
Reading
Instruction

Susan E. Israel

INTERNATIONAL
Reading Association
800 BARKSDALE ROAD, PO BOX 8139
NEWARK, DE 19714-8139, USA
www.reading.org

The International Reading Association attempts, through its publications, to provide a forum for a wide spectrum of opinions on reading. This policy permits divergent viewpoints without implying the endorsement of the Association.

Executive Editor, Books Corinne M. Mooney
Developmental Editor Charlene M. Nichols
Developmental Editor Tori Mello Bachman
Developmental Editor Stacey Lynn Sharp
Editorial Production Manager Shannon T. Fortner
Design and Composition Manager Anette Schuetz

Project Editors Stacey Lynn Sharp and Cynthia L. Held

Art Cover Design, Lise Holliker Dykes; Cover Photo, © Image Source Limited; Interior Illustrations, © Jupiter Images Corporation

Library of Congress Cataloging-in-Publication Data

Israel, Susan E.
  Using metacognitive assessments to create individualized reading instruction / Susan E. Israel.
    p. cm.
  Includes bibliographical references and index.
  ISBN 978-0-87207-621-1
  1. Individualized reading instruction. 2. Reading (Elementary) 3. Metacognition in children. I. Title.
  LB1573.45.I77 2007
  372.41'7--dc22

2007027898

This book is dedicated to my father-in-law, Richard Israel, for his support and encouragement to publish and devote myself to something I love.

CONTENTS

Susan E. Israel, PhD, is an assistant professor in the field of reading and educational psychology. Her research agenda focuses on reading comprehension and child–mind development as it relates to literacy processes in reading and writing. Israel became interested in metacognitive instruction when she was a language arts teacher, and her dissertation focused on metacognitive strategy instruction across text types and reading levels. More recently, Israel has used metacognitive assessments in her experience as a literacy coach and includes metacognitive assessments in her graduate-level reading and diagnostics courses.

Israel was awarded the 2005 Panhellenic Council Outstanding Professor Award at the University of Dayton, Ohio, USA. She was also the 1998 recipient of the Teacher as Researcher Grant from the International Reading Association (IRA), for which she has served and been a member for more than a decade.

Her most recent publications include an edited volume with E. Jennifer Monaghan titled *Shaping the Reading Field: The Impact of Early Reading Pioneers, Scientific Research, and Progressive Ideas* (IRA, 2007) and an edited volume with Michelle M. Israel titled *Poetic Possibilities: Poems to Enhance Literacy Learning* (IRA, 2006), which features poems from *The Reading Teacher*. She is also coeditor with Gerald G. Duffy of the upcoming volume on reading comprehension titled *Handbook of Research on Reading Comprehension* (Taylor & Francis [formerly Erlbaum], in press). Currently, she is integrating her research to explore publishing opportunities in the area of children's literature and young adult fiction and nonfiction.

When she is not researching or writing, she spends time working in her garden and is busy making quilts.

Author Information for Correspondence and Workshops
Israel would enjoy hearing from those who have found *Using Metacognitive Assessments to Create Individualized Reading Instruction* useful in their teaching. She may be contacted at sueisrael@insightbb.com.

FOREWORD

I t is a pleasure and a privilege to write the foreword to *Using Metacognitive Assessments to Create Individualized Reading Instruction* by Susan E. Israel. One of my enduring interests as an applied developmental psychologist is how research on children's learning is translated into practice in educational settings. To complement my own research on the development of metacognition, I have been keeping up with the articles and books written for classroom teachers on how to foster and assess metacognition. A variety of assessment approaches originally used in research have been recommended to teachers, including interviews, questionnaires, think-alouds, error detection procedures, anecdotal records and observations, and student self-assessment. Unfortunately, these approaches are often described in such general terms that they cannot easily be put into place in the classroom. Worse yet, many times the assessments are presented without alerting teachers to their limitations and the conditions of appropriate use.

Therefore, I was delighted to learn that this book had been written, and it was with a great deal of enthusiasm that I read it. For the first time, teachers now have an excellent and comprehensive source of information on how to assess the metacognitive skills of their students and how to use that assessment information to guide their reading instruction. The practical recommendations that Susan Israel offers are strongly grounded in research, and you will come away from this book knowing how, when, and why to use the assessment tools she describes so effectively. I trust you will find this book a valuable resource that you return to again and again.

—*Linda Baker*
University of Maryland, Baltimore County

PREFACE

Using *Metacognitive Assessments to Create Individualized Reading Instruction* is a resource for literacy educators who want to understand how to use assessments to enhance literacy skills using metacognitive approaches. As a literacy professor who teaches undergraduate- and graduate-level reading courses, I am often asked to recommend a book that specifically helps teachers understand how to assess and teach metacognition. Teachers have expressed to me the need for a resource that guides them on how to understand students' thoughts about their reading ability and better integrate metacognition and strategies in reading instruction. This book was written in response to that request.

This book expands on my first book on metacognition, *Metacognition in Literacy Learning* (2005), by focusing specifically on metacognitive assessments and providing literacy teachers with the assessment tools needed to understand students' metacognitive ability. While *Metacognition in Literacy Learning* sets the stage for understanding metacognition from a theoretical perspective and summarizes the research on all aspects of metacognition, this book places emphasis on assessment administration prior to instruction in order to understand students' metacognitive abilities. The book then builds on the idea of metacognitive assessments as a way to guide instruction relative to individual student needs.

My experience in teaching metacognitively oriented strategies with the goal of developing self-regulated readers and increasing reading comprehension began when I was a fourth-grade language arts teacher. One of the textbooks I read for my graduate-level reading course was *Windows Into Literacy: Assessing Learners, K–8* by Rhodes and Shanklin (1993). *Windows Into Literacy* helped explain the concepts of Flavell's (1979) early research on metacognition and put them into context with reading. Administering reading and writing inventories and integrating self-assessments to understand reading-related activities was considered innovative practice at the time I began my graduate studies in metacognitive-oriented reading instruction. Today, metacognition and reading comprehension are a common part of reading education curricula and should be common practice with literacy educators at all levels.

My first experiences with using self-assessments occurred when I was a classroom teacher. The self-assessments gave me insight into various levels of developmental issues related to metacognitive knowledge. I realized that not all students had the ability to think metacognitively, and I had to strengthen this way of thinking through my instruction.

As I continued using various metacognitive assessments and strategies in my classroom, I realized that I wanted to learn more about the current research related to metacognitive ability. This desire became the focus of my dissertation, which was on verbal protocol analysis and conscious constructive responses of students at various reading levels. The creation of this book stems from my research in using metacognitive assessments and my experiences using them as a classroom teacher and assistant professor. I wrote this book out of a desire for classroom teachers to have easy access to different types of metacognitive assessments and a practical understanding of how to use them to create individualized reading instruction. I used many of the assessments in this book to help my preservice and inservice teachers with classroom assessments and diagnostics.

Who Should Read This Book

The recommended audience for this book is any elementary school literacy or reading educator. This book is also a valuable resource for preservice and practicing teachers who want to understand metacognition and how to use metacognitive assessments to increase literacy achievement. Reading specialists, literacy coaches, content area teachers, and teacher educators will also benefit from the information presented in this resource.

Classroom teachers will benefit from reading this book because the format and contents are organized for the teacher who wants to learn about all aspects of metacognition and integrate the practical applications supported by research. Each chapter scaffolds educators through a diagnostic and intervention framework that develops metacognitively skilled readers.

Reading specialists or literacy coaches will find a variety of metacognitive assessments that can be easily implemented in classrooms and learn about research-based metacognitive strategies that can be adapted to a variety of situations and with students at varying levels of reading ability.

Content area teachers will find the information on metacognitive assessments helpful in obtaining information about the reading skills of students reading expository and informational texts that may not engage readers and develop efficient comprehension. This book is also a valuable cognitive building tool for teachers who wish to develop metacognitive thinking in content areas.

University professors who teach reading courses will appreciate this book's handbook format and having a resource to enhance curriculum in undergraduate-level and graduate-level reading courses. Because few programs in higher education offer a course on reading comprehension and metacognition, reading courses have to be designed to integrate mini-units devoted to topics of metacognition and reading comprehension. This book can be used as a supplemental resource to guide preservice and inservice teachers on how to use assessments and research-based practices related to developing metacognition and reading comprehension in classroom situations.

How to Use This Book

The Introduction to this book provides a solid understanding of foundational information related to metacognition and metacognitive thinking, explaining the connection between metacognition and reading, functions of metacognition, and metacognitive strategy utilization before, during, and after reading. Then, the book is organized into five chapters. Chapter 1 builds on this understanding by exploring metacognitive assessments and their role in metacognitive-oriented reading instruction, placing metacognitive assessments in context with metacognitive instruction. The chapter details the principles and student and teacher benefits of using metacognitive assessments. Chapter 2 shows you how to get started with using metacognitive assessments in metacognitive-oriented reading instruction by using goal-setting strategies, providing in lesson plan format many practical activities on goal setting and planning as a way to introduce students to metacognitive thinking.

Chapters 3–5 focus on three types of metacognitive assessments that will help teachers at all levels. Chapter 3 focuses on interviews and the process of conducting interviews to obtain information about students' metacognitive awareness and strategy utilization. Chapter 4 focuses on surveys and inventories. In this chapter, you will find several different types of metacognitive assessments that can be administered to larger groups or on an individual basis. In chapter 5 think-alouds and the procedures for conducting think-alouds are explained.

The appendixes to this book provide teachers with reproducible forms (see Appendix A) and access to well known metacognitive assessment tools (see Appendix B) so that teachers have a ready available resource of assessments to choose from.

The resulting benefit to literacy teachers is understanding the needs of readers with the goal of providing individualized instruction that develops metacognitively skilled readers.

This book is written to offer a readable, practical, yet research-based text using the following writing style features:

- The format enhances readability and understanding of key concepts.
- The language of the entire book is based on research but is presented in a concise and straightforward manner that is not intimidating for readers.

• The metacognitive assessments are explained using teacher-friendly examples that are research oriented.

It is important to note that teachers should not use the instructional material or metacognitive assessments offered in this book in a linear fashion or perceive this material strictly as recipes to follow in order to improve reading comprehension. It is conceptually more effective to organize the strategies into meaningful pockets and then use the information in this book to help you refine or redefine your pedagogy. When reading this book ask yourself questions such as, How does this apply to my teaching situation? What can I learn here in order to improve my instruction? Will using metacognitive assessments help me individualize reading instruction for my students, and if so, how? If not, what can I do to learn from this information so that I can improve instruction? It would also be helpful to keep a journal of your reflections as you read in order to help you directly apply the knowledge gained through reading this book to your individual students and classrooms.

The following section outlines additional special features that enhance the readability and practicality of this book.

Chapter Goals

Each chapter begins with an outline of Chapter Goals, which ties key ideas of the chapter together and allows you to read with purpose. The Chapter Goals can also be used as a way to organize the text while reading the chapter.

Classroom Scenarios

Classroom Scenarios appear throughout each chapter in order to provide practical applications of the content and research base presented. This feature helps the reader make connections with the chapter's contents and understand how that content is integrated into classrooms. The Classroom Scenarios also highlight everyday situations that reading teachers in all classrooms may encounter. This feature will help teachers reflect on their practice.

Resources to Enrich Your Understanding

At the end of the chapters, the Resources to Enrich Your Understanding feature identifies resources on specific topics of interest and is organized around key concepts in the chapter. This feature helps the reader focus on professional development resources that target specific areas. These lists can also be used for small professional development groups that aim to improve instruction and focus on using metacognitive assessments as tools for effective individualized instruction.

Acknowledgments

The completion of this manuscript is largely due to the expertise of Corinne Mooney, Executive Editor, Books, for the International Reading Association. Corinne's dedication was reflected in her ability to motivate using positive feedback and encouragement. I would also like to thank Developmental Editor Stacey Sharp and Production Editor Cindy Held, who responded to my many questions about the editing and production of the manuscript.

Permissions Granted

The success of this book is also due to the publishers who granted permission to reprint some of the metacognitive assessments that are included in the book—the International Reading Association, Routledge (formerly Erlbaum), Henry Holt and Company, and the American Psychological Association.

I especially want to thank the following assessment authors for giving me permission to reprint their assessments:

- Scott Paris, for permission to reprint the Index of Reading Awareness
- Vincent Miholic, for permission to reprint the Reading Strategy Awareness Inventory
- Kouider Mokhtari and Carla Reichard, for permission to reprint the Metacognitive Awareness of Reading Strategies Inventory (MARSI)
- Maribeth Cassidy Schmitt, for permission to reprint the Metacomprehension Strategy Index
- Peter Afflerbach and K.W. Meuwissen, for permission to reprint the Differentiated Analytic Reading Self-Assessment

Thinking Metacognitively

CHAPTER GOALS

- Become familiar with metacognitive thinking by learning about current research on metacognition and metacognitive processes.
- Reflect on metacognitive-oriented reading instruction by understanding metacognitive strategies during developmental stages.
- Contextualize the relationship between metacognitive strategies and pedagogy.

Metacognition is a critical aspect of effective reading and reading instruction, and before using metacognitive assessments as a tool to create individualized instruction in your classroom, it is important to possess a solid understanding of what metacognition is and why metacognitive strategies are, in fact, such an integral part of effective reading. Therefore, in order to help reading professionals understand why metacognition and metacognitive strategies should be integrated into reading instruction, this chapter provides a straightforward introduction to the connection between metacognition and reading comprehension, a description of some of the theoretical aspects of metacognition, an exploration of pedagogy that develops metacognition, and an explanation of how increasing metacognitive awareness has a direct impact on reading comprehension and motivation and the development of self-regulated readers. The chapter also provides an overview of the functions of metacognition, the developmental levels at which metacognitive strategy utilization occurs, and recommended phases for introducing metacognitive strategies to students.

What Is Metacognition?

Metacognition is defined as thinking about one's thoughts (Harris & Hodges, 1995); in other words, it is a cognitive process where one is aware of his or her own thinking. As you are reading this chapter, you may be thinking to yourself,

Why is the concept of metacognition important to teaching and literacy learning? You might also be thinking about what you know—or do not know—about metacognition and considering whether the concepts in this book will be difficult to understand, let alone implement in the classroom. However, the fact that you are thinking about this book, your level of understanding, and how to utilize the assessment resources to increase reading ability with your students *is* metacognitive thinking. You are making an evaluation of the book while at the same time activating your prior knowledge. You are also asking yourself questions. Is this book for me? How will this book help my students? How will I use metacognitive assessments with my students to understand their literacy levels? When you ask yourself these questions you are illustrating metacognition as you think about your own thinking.

As an educator, you likely already have an advanced level of metacognitive thinking by virtue of teacher education and training in reflective analysis. Your professional development resources have challenged you to think about your instruction in a way that improves student learning. However, it is not only important for teachers to be metacognitive thinkers, it is also important for students to think metacognitively.

Can metacognitive strategies be taught? When I spoke with my preservice and inservice teachers about metacognition, I was surprised to learn of the misconception that metacognition could not be taught in the classroom, that it was something achieved through experience and only with superior cognitive ability. In addition, many of these preservice and inservice teachers believed that it could only be developed later in life. However, Flavell (1979) and many other researchers—such as Paris, Baker, Palincsar, and Pressley—have since supported the idea that "Increasing the quantity and quality of children's metacognitive knowledge and monitoring skills through systematic training may be feasible as well as desirable" (Flavell, p. 906).

The Connection Between Metacognition and Reading Comprehension

How is metacognition related to reading? The initial introduction of metacognition into reading was by Myers and Paris in 1978 with their research about children's metacognitive knowledge and awareness of reading. Early research on metacognition conducted during the 1970s and 1980s launched the expedition into further research on how teaching metacognition and metacognitive strategies can be integrated in the curriculum to enhance reading comprehension (Baker & Brown, 1984; Flavell, 1979; Myers & Paris, 1978). The transition of the concept of metacognition from cognitive psychology to educational psychology to reading education happened gradually. Acknowledgment for much of what we now know goes to subsequent research conducted by Garner (Garner & Reis, 1981; Garner & Taylor, 1982), Paris (Paris & Flukes, 2005; Paris & Paris, 2003; Paris & Stahl, 2005), Baker (Baker & Anderson, 1982), Palincsar (Palincsar & Brown, 1984), Pressley (Pressley, Brown, El-Dinary, & Afflerbach, 1995), and others.

Much of the early research utilizing metacognitive assessment tools in the area of verbal protocol analysis became the foundation for what we now know about reading processes. In their landmark study on reading behaviors of good readers, Pressley and Afflerbach (1995) found that expert readers and highly skilled readers use specific metacognitive strategies before, during, and after reading to aid in their comprehension and understanding of the texts being read. The behaviors that good readers use help them to construct meaning while reading, make evaluations of text, and make connections with prior knowledge and experiences. In fact, effective readers apply these strategies automatically. *Automaticity* is the function of performing a task with little attention or thinking, and metacognitvely skilled readers have internalized the ability to utilize effective reading strategies when comprehending text so that they are able to utilize these strategies automatically (Laberge & Samuels, 1974). Less able readers are less proficient in automatically applying metacognitive strategies and, therefore, teachers will need to teach the strategies (Block & Israel, 2004; Pressley & Afflerbach, 1995). Evidence supports that it is essential for exemplary literacy teachers to integrate metacognitive teaching strategies in their literacy instruction at all grade levels and assist students in becoming independent self-regulated readers through the utilization of metacognitive strategy applications (Block & Mangieri, 2004).

More recently, Baker (2005), who researches in the area of metacognitive development, did a thorough evaluation of the developmental differences in metacognition and the implications for metacognitive-oriented reading instruction, which can be found in *Metacognition in Literacy Learning* (Israel, Block, Bauserman, & Kinnucan-Welsch, 2005). Baker explains the implications for metacognitively oriented reading instruction, stating that "metacognitive skills should be taught within the context of authentic literacy engagement, and students should be given sufficient practice in their application that they know when, why, and how to use them relatively effortlessly" (p. 74).

Metacognitive strategies increase readers' meaning construction, monitoring of text and reading comprehension, and their ability to evaluate the text they are reading. Metacognitively skilled readers are readers who are aware of knowledge, procedures, and controls of the reading process. They use this knowledge during the reading process to improve reading and comprehension ability. Table 1

Table 1. Contextualizing the Language of Metacognition With Literacy Instruction

Metacognitive Term	Definition	What This Term Might Look Like in the Classroom	Why Teachers Integrate the Strategy in Literacy Instruction
Automaticity	Performing a task without thinking or with little attention	Students are able to decode text without hesitation when they come to unknown words.	Teachers want students to read automatically; therefore, helping students be able to decode words would be valued.
Conscious Constructive Responses	Conscious processes carried out by good readers to help increase comprehension (Pressley & Afflerbach, 1995)	Good reading behaviors are exhibited consciously when used to obtain meaning before, during, and after reading.	Teachers want students to model good reading behaviors. In order for students to become knowledgeable about good reading strategies students need effective instruction.
Comprehension Monitoring	The noting of one's successes and failures in developing or attaining meaning, usually with reference to an emerging conception of the meaning of the text as a whole, and adjusting one's reading processes accordingly	A student stumbles when encountering a word that is unknown while reading, and rather than skipping the word and continuing reading, a good reader will utilize monitoring strategies to stop and try to discover the meaning of the unknown word.	In order for students of all ages to become more self-regulated and improve reading comprehension, students need to possess strategies that helps them monitor their own reading comprehension in order to develop into life long readers.
Metacognitive Strategies	Tools to help develop thinking processes and include control over reading (Israel, Block, Bauserman, and Kinnucan-Welsch, 2005)	A teacher helps increase students' reading comprehension when reading a story by modeling different types of planning, monitoring, and evaluation strategies.	The purpose of integrating metacognitive strategies with reading instruction is to improve reading comprehension and develop more effective and critical readers.
Self-Regulation	Setting realistic goals, employing strategies to achieve the goals, closely monitoring their attainment, and evaluating one's own thinking	Prior to reading a story, the reader is able to answer the question, "What is your purpose for reading this story."	Allowing students opportunities to be more in charge of their reading processes improves reading achievement.

(continued)

Table 1. Contextualizing the Language of Metacognition With Literacy Instruction (continued)

Metacognitive Term	Definition	What This Term Might Look Like in the Classroom	Why Teachers Integrate the Strategy in Literacy Instruction
Think-Aloud	A metacognitive strategy that can be used as an assessment in which cognitive thought processes are verbalized (Block & Israel, 2004; Israel, 2002)	When reading a nonfiction text, the teacher stops after the first few pages and says, "This story reminds me of a time I..." The teacher continues to read the story and stops when something is not clear. The teacher might say, "Why did the character..."	Teaching to develop metacognitive thinking helps develop skilled readers. Verbalizing ones thoughts provides information about the student's cognitive processes. Skilled teachers will use this information to understand the reader.

provides an overview of important terms that teachers can use to help them contextualize the language of metacognition and literacy instruction. This table is useful because it provides a visual image of what the term might look like in the classroom as well as the rationale for why teachers should integrate metacognitive thinking in the classroom.

Learning About Metacognitive Functions

There are three primary functions of metacognition: knowledge, procedural, and executive (Flavell, 1979). *Knowledge* refers to an understanding of metacognitive skills and strategies. Knowing when and how to perform metacognitive strategies defines the *executive* function of metacognition. *Procedural* functions of metacognition allow the reader to understand how to perform the strategies and then actually execute the strategies without thinking. For example, when a student successfully uses the monitoring strategy for reading comprehension, the following functions would be exhibited:

- The reader understands that monitoring is a strategy that requires him or her to rethink and question what has been understood (knowledge function).
- The reader recognizes why the monitoring strategy should be used and the appropriate times to use this strategy during the reading (executive function).

• The reader is able to utilize the text content in order to use the monitoring strategy (procedural function).

This reader understands how to use the monitoring strategy when there might be a contradiction within the text or a breakdown in his or her comprehension (Israel et al., 2005).

Table 2 presents an overview of the behaviors students exhibit for each of the three primary functions of metacognition. This table will help teachers identify when students are applying metacognitive functions. It is important for teachers to be able to identify these metacognitive functions as students exhibit them so that they can have a better understanding of how to interpret and apply the appropriate metacognitive assessments and strategies with their students. In addition, knowing the functions of metacognition will help place the developmental levels of metacognition into perspective with appropriate strategies that can be taught.

Metacognitive Strategy Utilization

Metacognitive strategies used to aid reading comprehension can be divided into three types: planning strategies (P), monitoring strategies (M), and evaluation

Table 2. Student Behaviors When Utilizing Metacognitive Functions

Behaviors Demonstrating the Knowledge Function	• Student is aware of strategies being used. • Student senses when there is a comprehension breakdown and makes an effort to correct. • Student is aware of reading habits. • Student understands the reading tasks and the necessary cognitive abilities to process text.
Behaviors Demonstrating the Executive Function	• Student understands when and why a specific strategy should be used and uses it. • Student executes task relevant strategies. • Student monitors use of strategies. • Student can explain which strategies he or she is using and why he or she is executing these strategies.
Behaviors Demonstrating the Procedural Function	• Student understands how to perform the various strategies involved. • Student performs strategies that help improve success with the task. • Student is able to model strategies for other students.

strategies (E) (Pressley & Afflerbach, 1995). This metacognitive reading frame-work should be familiar to teachers who integrate before-, during-, and after-reading processes when teaching students effective comprehension strategies (Pressley & Afflerbach, 1995).

Planning Strategies

Planning strategies are metacognitive strategies that the reader does early on in the reading process—before reading—to increase reading comprehension. The following planning strategies are utilized by metacognitive readers **before** reading:

- Activating Prior Knowledge
- Overviewing Information in the Text
- Relating Text-to-Text
- Relating Text-to-Self

Monitoring Strategies

Monitoring strategies—usually occurring during the reading of a text—help the reader pay attention to meaning construction as well as correct breakdowns in comprehension. The following monitoring strategies are utilized by metacognitive readers **during** reading:

- Determining Word Meaning
- Questioning
- Reflecting
- Monitoring
- Summarizing
- Looking for Important Information

Evaluating Strategies

Evaluation strategies—used after reading—allow the reader to think critically about the text and make a cognitive or affective judgment. The following evaluating strategies are utilized by metacognitive readers **after** reading:

- Thinking Like the Author
- Evaluating the Text
- Anticipating Use of Knowledge

A student in your class is not reading the required text. You suspect that he might be having difficulty paying attention to what he is reading because he is unable to relate to the topic and therefore does not engage with the text. As a teacher, you want to understand why he is not reading, and the student explains to you that he does not understand the text because he does not know anything about the topic.

Sit with him and a small group of other students who might also be having trouble and model for them how you would use some planning strategies prior to reading. For example, one often overlooked metacognitive strategy is Overviewing Information in the Text before reading. Model for students how to look over the book to get an idea what the book is about and how to look for important information in the book and explain why you think this information might be important to know or remember. In addition, point out text features, such as the table of contents, index, any information about the author, and the publication date. Then model the Activating Prior Knowledge strategy by discussing with the students any prior experiences you might have with the text and help students understand how important it is to activate their prior knowledge. Trying new strategies and making this student and other students feel like their experiences are important is key to getting students' attention.

Understanding Metacognitive Strategies Effective at Developmental Stages

Teachers should understand that development plays a key role in metacognition (Samuels, Ediger, Willcutt, & Palumbo, 2005). This is important because, in order for students to develop metacognitive strategies, teachers need to be attentive to students' literacy learning levels and reading abilities so that they can teach metacognitive strategies suited to students' individual ability levels. Using metacognitive assessments will help teachers understand students' metacognitive abilities in order to guide students to increased levels of automatic metacognitive strategy utilization.

Even at the preschool and elementary school level, children are already developing metacognitive strategies by asking questions. Young children's natural inquisitiveness helps them make sense of their world. Therefore, parents play a large role in the initial development of strategy utilization. When reading stories to children, parents often ask the child questions about the book, and in return, the child also asks questions. Sometimes the questions might seem irrelevant to the text, but young children attempt to place the content of the story within the context of their personal experiences or knowledge base. Children activate schema, which is important when developing metacognitive strategies, and by reflecting on prior experiences, children develop metacognitive thinking.

Therefore, one way teachers and parents of young learners can help develop their metacognitive thinking is to use a one-question assessment strategy: Why? Constantly asking children to explain their thinking helps them develop connections with their prior knowledge and experiences. As children begin to read on their own, they will ask themselves "why" questions automatically.

In the upper elementary grades, students begin to develop good reading behaviors. Through reading experiences and opportunities to learn metacognitive strategies, they can increase their levels of reading comprehension ability. They are capable of using strategies more independently without teacher prompting when given the opportunity to do so. Organization of text structures is very important to readers at this level. In addition, readers will always ask questions about why this information is important to them or why they should do the required task. Although this might appear to be complaining, the reader is actually activating a metacognitive strategy of evaluation. He or she wants to know what value the information will have in the future.

In summary, in the primary grades "other regulation" leads to "self-regulation." Self-regulation leads to the development of the metacognitive ability to self-assess. If children are taught when, where, and why particular strategies for word recognition are valuable, students can begin to develop the foundational literacy skills that will lead to metacognitive-oriented reading. If students are having problems with reading comprehension, encouraging the application of metacognitive strategies can help to provide pathways to self-correction during oral and silent reading. In addition, teaching children to reflect on the processes and strategies they use before, during, and after reading will also help developing or less proficient readers understand the mental processes used when making sense of text. Even as early as the preschool years, children use strategies they understand and can verbalize how to use them. Reading research on metacognition has helped educators at all levels understand what types of strategies we can expect students to be capable of learning.

Table 3 offers a summary of the metacognitive strategies that can be developed and enhanced through instruction in the primary and upper elementary grades. The table illustrates that metacognitive strategies can be taught at all levels, although at varying degrees of intensity.

Table 3. Summary of Metacognitive Strategies by Level

Level	Type	Metacognitive Strategies
Primary Grades	Planning	*Activating Prior Knowledge*: Relating text to reader's own prior life experiences and knowledge
		Overviewing Information in the Text: Overviewing the text to make sense of the topic, format, and key concepts
	Monitoring	*Determining Word Meaning*: Identifying terms or concepts that might be confusing
		Questioning: Asking questions while reading and questioning the information presented, such as Why? and How does this make sense?
		Reflecting: Reflecting on textual elements or things that puzzle them
	Evaluating	*Thinking Like the Author*: Beginning to understand authors' perspectives
		Evaluating the Text: Beginning to analyze texts by expressing thoughts such as "I like this because..."
Upper Elementary Grades	Planning	*Relating Text-to-Text*: Comparing ideas within the text for consistency and activating prior knowledge of texts
		Relating Text-to-Self: Using information in the text to activate prior experiences
	Monitoring	*Monitoring*: Understanding when there is breakdown in comprehension and using fix-up strategies to correct
		Summarizing: Stating key concepts or events from the text
		Looking for Important Information: Finding important information in the text that will aid in increased levels of understanding, activation of prior knowledge, and increased concentration based on the perceived levels of importance to reading goals
	Evaluating	*Anticipating Use of Knowledge*: Understanding how to use knowledge in the future
		Evaluating the Text: Thinking about how this text made you feel (e.g., asking yourself, Was the information valuable to you? How can you use this information in the future. Would you recommend this to someone else and if so, why?)

Phases for Introducing Metacognitive Reading Strategies in the Classroom

There are three phases of how metacognitively oriented reading strategies can be introduced in order to increase internalization of strategies. Figure 1 explains the three phases of instruction that lead to metacognitively skilled readers. Teachers can follow the phases when introducing metacognitive strategies.

Figure 1. Phases of Metacognitively Oriented Reading Instruction

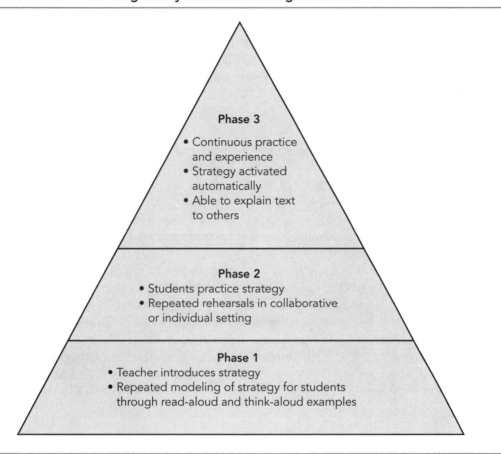

Phase 3
- Continuous practice and experience
- Strategy activated automatically
- Able to explain text to others

Phase 2
- Students practice strategy
- Repeated rehearsals in collaborative or individual setting

Phase 1
- Teacher introduces strategy
- Repeated modeling of strategy for students through read-aloud and think-aloud examples

Phase 1

After being first introduced to a strategy, students are not yet able to use it spontaneously. A common pitfall of strategy instruction is that teachers may expect students to learn a strategy that has only been presented once. Students need to feel confident about strategy utilization. Increase confidence levels by repeated introductions in a variety of situations.

Phase 2

In this phase, students are able to use the strategy with practice, but they do not initially benefit from the strategy. Teachers should not assume that, with only a little practice and successful demonstration on a worksheet, the student has acquired the skill. I have seen many exemplary teachers avoid sending homework home on the first day after a new strategy has been introduced.

Phase 3

It is not until the third phase on the learning continuum and after students have had considerable practice and experience with using the strategy that spontaneous utilization occurs. At this phase, students are closer to being metacognitively skilled readers and will feel more confident about doing practice exercises.

CLASSROOM SCENARIO: Transferring Strategies Across Text Types

A student in your class successfully demonstrates the utilization of a metacognitive reading strategy when reading a fictional text but is unsuccessful at transferring the strategy when reading in nonfiction textbook in science class. How can you change your instruction or selection of read-alouds to help students learn how to transfer strategies from one text type to another?

If a student is having trouble applying the strategies to nonfiction text, evaluate the types of text being used during your read-aloud experiences to model strategy utilization. If you are only using fiction text, you should incorporate more nonfiction text (illustrating Phase 1 of introducing students to metacognitive reading strategies). In addition, you should practice using a variety of text types with students (illustrating Phase 2). You can monitor strategy utilization by evaluating reading comprehension using metacognitive assessments in chapters 3 through 5 of this book (illustrating Phase 3).

Conclusion

This chapter provides the foundational information needed to develop a solid understanding of the meaning of metacognition, how metacognition is related to reading instruction, and the functions of metacognition. In addition, this chapter introduces key metacognitive strategies used by effective readers and the different stages at which these metacognitive strategies can be introduced. Now that you are equipped with a solid background on metacognition and metacognitive reading strategies, you are ready to move on to chapter 1, in which you will be introduced to metacognitive assessments and the purposes and benefits of metacognitive assessments.

Resources to Enrich Your Understanding

I first encountered the concept of metacognition in the book *Mosaic of Thought* (Keene & Zimmermann, 1997). I have used this book in my classes as a book study selection, and it is always one of the more popular choices for both undergraduate and graduate students. Even though the book was written in 1997, reading educators will find the text to be inspiring, as well as a motivation for instructional change. If more information is needed on any of the topics or research in this chapter, I recommend reading *Metacognition in Literacy Learning* (Israel, Block, et al., 2005). A valuable chapter in this book that discusses developmental differences is "Developmental Differences in Metacognition: Implications for Metacognitively Oriented Reading Instruction." More and more teachers are using picture books as tools for increased literacy development. Two of my favorite picture books that emphasize metacognitive thinking use creative language to get kids thinking. When I traveled to Ireland during the summer of 2004, I asked the bookstores what their bestselling picture book is, and I was given *The Gruffalo*, by Julia Donaldson (1999). This book was awarded the Smarties Book Prize in Ireland for outstanding literature. The story begins, "A mouse took a stroll through the deep dark wood. A fox saw the mouse and the mouse looked good." Teachers at all levels can use this book to teach monitoring strategies. The story is so good that children will immediately request a reread to confirm comprehension. Kaethe Zemach (1998) wrote an excellent story titled *The Character in the Book*. Because the story is written in the character's perspective, children need to think metacognitively.

CHAPTER 1

Understanding Metacognitive Assessments

CHAPTER GOALS

- Become familiar with what metacognitive assessments are and what they measure.
- Understand how and why metacognitive assessments can be used as a method to guide individualized instruction.
- Recognize the principles of metacognitive assessments and how to apply overarching principles to successfully organize metacognitive-oriented reading instruction and the administration of metacognitive assessments.

In the Introduction, you became familiar with the concept of metacognition and the foundations of metacognitive-oriented reading instruction. You now have a broader understanding of metacognitive strategy utilization and awareness of strategies that good readers use before, during, and after reading experiences. You also learned about general developmental characteristics for primary-grade and upper elementary school students regarding metacognitive strategy utilization and understand that each student's range of strategy utilization varies based on his or her cognitive ability and reading experiences. This means that teachers should be knowledgeable about both metacognitive strategies and individual students' capabilities prior to creating individualized reading instruction.

The purpose of this chapter is to help you move from understanding basic tenets of metacognition to learning about the principles of metacognitive assessments and how they can be conceptually applied in the classroom. First, you will be introduced to the basic concepts of metacognitive assessments and the rationale that supports the use of metacognitive assessments to create individualized reading instruction. Then five principles are defined and explained in relationship to the organization and selection of metacognitive assessments. Following this explanation is a more detailed summary of what teachers—

regardless of experience levels—need to know, how teachers can apply the principle with classroom practices, and what teachers can do to avoid implementing principles inappropriately. Additional research is included to add depth to each principle and provide further information about how the conceptual importance of each principle is applied in terms of instructional interventions and outcomes.

What Are Metacognitive Assessments?

Metacognitive assessments are measures that evaluate the level and utilization of thinking processes or strategies, as well as what the reader is thinking related to reading tasks and behaviors (Harris & Hodges, 1995; Paris & Flukes, 2005). In other words, metacognitive assessments allow teachers to "get into the mind" of students as they read and understand students' conscious constructive responses to reading processes and reading behaviors. As part of metacognitive-oriented reading instruction, teachers can use metacognitive assessments as a tool to gain valuable information about students in order to guide individual instruction. Metacognitive assessments are valuable tools that aid teachers in identifying cognitive ability, as well as cognitive misunderstandings, so that students can receive more effective and more appropriate literacy instruction (Israel, Bauserman, & Block, 2005). Because metacognitive strategies can be taught and they improve comprehension, assessing metacognitive ability should be the goal of all teachers (Sweet & Snow, 2003). According to Paris and Flukes (2005), who summarized the existing research on metacognitive assessments, there are three types of research-based metacognitive assessments: interviews (discussed in chapter 3), surveys and inventories (discussed in chapter 4), and think-alouds (discussed in chapter 5).

Metacognitive Assessments: Moving From Theory to Practice

Because of current shifts in literacy instruction due to No Child Left Behind Act and Reading First initiatives, teachers are challenged to consider the value of metacognitive assessments as tools to understanding reading behaviors in order to meet the literacy needs of all learners. By allowing teachers to learn more about the level and utilization of thinking processes or strategies that students exhibit while reading, metacognitive assessment tools aid in the development of reflective and self-regulated readers (Israel, Bauserman, et al., 2005; Israel, Block, et al., 2005; Pressley & Afflerbach, 1995). According to Block (2004), one of the weakest areas of instruction in elementary school classrooms is the amount of time spent on developing self-regulated readers:

> To date, we have not developed enough programs to promote metacognition, much less the assessment instruments that can be used to measure their success. We must examine more curricula and evaluative tools empirically. There is an equal need to identify the factors that contribute to the speed with which above, on, and below grade level students become automatic, metacognitive readers. Do students of variant reading ability levels require different instructional methods to build life-long automatic use of metacognitive thinking? (p. 85)

As discussed in the Introduction, we now know that metacognition is a powerful force behind increasing comprehension during reading tasks (Block, 2004; Block & Pressley, 2002). Knowing more about reading behaviors, attitudes, and perceptions through metacognitive assessments enables teachers to understand more about student's reading abilities, which provides teachers with the knowledge to more effectively tailor reading instruction for individual students and individual needs. Further, in addition to using the results of metacognitive assessments to individualize instruction for students, teachers can use the results of these assessments to cater to the needs of at-risk students—or any students— who are struggling with specific aspects of reading, such as comprehension, and therefore the repetition of repeated skills already learned can be avoided. Students will then receive more effective reading instruction, guiding them toward becoming effective and self-regulated readers In addition to developing a reflective attitude and increased levels of awareness about their own reading behaviors, metacognitive assessments allow students to have a better understanding of which strategies they are comfortable using and which strategies would influence increased levels of reading ability if further developed. Student benefits of metacognitive assessments are key to why teachers should read this book and implement metacognitive assessments in classroom practice.

So how are metacognitive assessments effective at helping students develop into better readers? How is literacy instruction that utilizes metacognitive assessments more effective than literacy instruction that does not assess students' metacognitive abilities? The answers to these questions are critical to understanding the rationale behind using metacognitive assessments to provide more effective and individualized literacy instruction. As Paris and Flukes (2005) state, "better understanding of what reading strategies are, and how they facilitate reading, and when and why they should be applied can help children overcome reading difficulties" (p. 122). Metacognitive assessments provide the necessary tools for teachers to gain a deeper understanding and appreciation for the strategies students are utilizing, as well as their awareness and beliefs about the strategies. Likewise, good readers effectively utilize metacognitive strategies in order to monitor their reading comprehension (Pressley & Afflerbach, 1995), and in order for students to effectively utilize metacognitive strategies they need to know what those strategies are (illustrating the knowledge function; see page 5 in the Introduction) and the purpose for using them (illustrating the procedural function; see page 5 in the Introduction). Metacognitive assessments aid in this understanding.

Another benefit of metacognitive assessments for students, according to Rhodes and Shanklin (1993), is that if teachers are going to individualize instruction for students, the planning of instruction needs to be based on the students' interpretations or reports: "Another important reason to assess metacognition is that student-centered instructional planning needs to take into the learner's point of view into account" (p. 111). Furthermore, in order for students to become self-regulated readers, they need to be knowledgeable about the reading process as well as how they go about engaging in strategic reading behaviors. Block, Gambrell, and Pressley (2002) emphasize the importance of students' awareness of the reading strategies they utilize during reading experiences. They state, "Researchers have confirmed what teachers of reading may have observed in themselves and in their students, namely, that thoughtful, active, proficient readers are metacognitive; they think about their own thinking during reading" (p. 84). Therefore, there is much to be gained from assessing metacognition with students, both from an instructional perspective and developmental perspective. If students are to grow in literacy development in order to become self-regulated and reflective readers, teachers have the moral obligation to help students achieve this goal.

CLASSROOM SCENARIO: Back-to-School Assessment Decisions

You are getting ready to start a new school year, and you do not have any information about your students' reading ability. What type of assessment can you use with the students' parents to gain more information about your new students? To gain an understanding of how your students' parents feel about their child's reading behaviors, use an open-ended questionnaire that asks three questions:

1. What do you think are your child's strengths related to reading?

2. What are areas for improvement related to reading?

3. What additional comments can you provide about your child and his or her literacy development?

Principles of Metacognitive Assessments

Paris and Flukes (2005) identified essential principles that define metacognitive assessments and their purposes. The five metacognitive assessment principles summarized in the section that follows are adapted from Paris and Flukes and written in the form of statements to help teachers reflect on assessment utilization and their application of reading strategies. A principle generally refers to the characteristics or assumption underlying the quality of a resource, and in this case the principles refer to classroom instruction and intervention based on the application of metacognitive assessments. Table 4 provides examples of classroom applications of each of the principles based on grade level. When selecting appropriate metacognitive measures to use with students, teachers should be familiar with the five principles so as to select and administer assessments in an appropriate and purposeful manner.

To aid teachers in maximizing their reading of this section, a reproducible planning guide integrating the five principles can be found on page 86 in Appendix A. This guide will assist you when selecting metacognitive assessments for your classroom. The planning guide can be used while reading this book to keep track of specific metacognitive assessments that will enhance your overall classroom literacy goals, and it will help you quickly identify which specific assessments you'd like to use in your instruction. As you are reading this book, you can use this guide to keep a record of metacognitive assessments that you would like to use with your students as well as the purpose for using the assessment so that you know when the assessment is appropriate to use (using the first and second columns of the guide). It may also be helpful to record the expected outcomes as you go (using the third column). Does the assessment target reading behaviors or reading strategies more specifically? You might also record what assessments work well with other assessments you are using or might choose to use in the future (using the fourth column) and which assessments are developmentally appropriate for your individual students (using the fifth column).

Principle #1

Metacognitive assessments should emphasize recurrent and comprehensive utilization of reading strategies.

When teachers select metacognitive assessments to administer, the metacognitive assessments should emphasize the utilization of learner-centered strategies so teachers can use the data from the assessments to create instruction that helps students transfer strategy utilization across text types and various reading tasks. Metacognitive assessments should not be limited to identifying strategy utilization

Table 4. Classroom Applications of Metacognitive Assessment Principles

Principles of Metacognitive Assessments	Application a Teacher Might Make in Primary Grades	Application a Teacher Might Make in Upper Elementary Grades
Principle #1: Metacognitive assessments should emphasize recurrent and comprehensive utilization of reading strategies.	During a read-aloud experience, the teacher asks, "What is your purpose for reading this book?"	When reading a difficult text, a teacher encourages students to stop at strategic points to evaluate their comprehension rather than continue reading whole chapters.
Principle #2: Metacognitive assessments measure the personal conceptions and perceived values of various reading strategies.	When a teacher is asking questions about the topic before reading in order to build prior knowledge, the teacher might also ask, "Does thinking about your prior experiences help you understand what you are reading?"	A teacher requests that while reading the passage, students keep track of how many times they use prior knowledge to help them understand what they are reading.
Principle #3: Metacognitive assessments should be developmentally appropriate and sensitive to students' progressive reading knowledge and proficiency levels.	At the beginning of the school year, the teacher asks the students to draw a picture of how reading makes them feel and explain what this picture means to them.	At the beginning of the school year, a teacher wants to finds out information about students' experiences with reading and uses a list of open-ended questions.
Principle #4: Metacognitive assessments should be used to complement existing measures of assessing reading fluency and comprehension.	A teacher uses a self-assessment after reading a story along with a list of comprehension questions.	A teacher uses a self-assessment before and after reading a story and asks students to explain all their answers. Students write their own comprehension questions and answer them.
Principle #5: Metacognitive assessments should be aligned with instructional goals so they provide diagnostic information about specific reading strategies.	A teacher wants to help students understand what to do when comprehension breaks down, so a strategy that asks them to evaluate the text with their prior knowledge is used.	A teacher wants to help students understand what to do when they lose comprehension, so a strategy that teaches them to go back and look for important information in the text, and asks them to evaluate the text in relationship with the text that might be confusing, is used.

Note. Principles adapted from Paris and Flukes (2005).

for only one genre, text type, or reading task. Instead, metacognitive assessments should be used to identify strategies that are valuable to students and that are utilized frequently. For example, younger students can be taught to overview the text by looking at textual features, an important strategy to use with fiction and nonfiction. Older children can also overview the text by looking at the textual features, and they can also look for important information that might be valuable to the overall comprehension of the text. Strategies that increase students' ability to relate their experiences to text being read are critical to developing early reading comprehension strategies. Strategies that students can transfer across disciplines (such as defining word meaning) should likewise be taught.

Determination of metacognitive assessment utilization requires teachers to have an understanding of the basic processes of reading and reading behaviors in conjunction with the students' needs. In addition, knowledge about comprehensive and recurrent grade-level strategies are vital information for purposeful and effective individualized instruction. August, Flavell, and Clift (1984) document the differences between skilled and less skilled readers relative to comprehension monitoring strategies. In this study, 15 fifth graders read five different stories on a computer screen. Researchers purposefully omitted a page of a few of the stories to see how the different groups would respond. Skilled readers significantly reported a page missing as opposed to less skilled readers because monitoring strategies were activated by the skilled readers. What teachers can learn from this study is the value of knowing individual students level of strategy utilization and how the strategy is being utilized across text types or print-rich material. This entails metacognitive assessments that emphasize frequency of monitoring strategy utilizations be used.

Necessary Background Information. Based on this principle, it is important for teachers to possess an understanding of the following key ideas before administering metacognitive assessments.

- Familiarity with strategies and how to effectively teach them is essential.
- A small group of strategies should be assessed and taught at a time.
- Instruction should include opportunities for students to transfer strategy utilization across text types.
- Knowing how assessment measures are administered is necessary prior to using with them with students.
- Assessments should be related to instructional goals.

How the Principle Can Be Applied in the Classroom. Based on Principle #1, some instructional recommendations for teachers when implementing metacognitive assessments include the following.

- Teach and assess skills that are related to instructional tasks.
- Explain to students how the small group of strategies are related and why they are learning them.
- Avoid teaching long lists of reading skills from prescribed reading programs.

Principle #2

Metacognitive assessments measure the personal conceptions and perceived values of various reading strategies.

Effective teachers use metacognitive assessments because they are sensitive to perceived values of their students. Perceived values are related to the level of importance a student places on specific strategies and whether or not the strategy is useful. Metacognitive assessments can effectively measure the following:

- Student's evaluation of strategy
- Frequency of usefulness
- Perceived strategy strengths
- Self-efficacy of strategy utilization

Therefore, it is important to analyze the assessments to obtain data that will help you better understand the emotions of your students and how the conscious response will affect cognitive ability. It is also important to ask students how and why they would use specific strategies. Effective teachers also ask students to compare the utilization of specific strategies and how they value the achieved outcomes when a specific strategy is activated.

In a research study that investigated reader beliefs and meaning construction in narrative text, Schraw (2000) found that transaction beliefs about reading—beliefs related to individual meanings of text for different readers—do affect comprehension, whereas transmission beliefs—beliefs related to the reader's understanding of the author's intended meaning—did not affect reading comprehension. Schraw concluded that the results of this study shed new light on the relationship between reader beliefs and understanding narrative text, stating, "Transaction beliefs appear to facilitate higher level meaning construction than transmission beliefs. However, these results may not apply when reading other text types" (p. 103). What teachers can learn from this study is that beliefs may influence student learning and teachers should take into account the reader's perceived beliefs.

Necessary Background Information. Based on this principle, it is important for teachers to possess an understanding of the following key ideas before administering metacognitive assessments.

- Student responses should be valued.
- Assessments that are not tied to a curriculum goal may cause students to respond inaccurately.
- It is important not to give criticism on communication of strategy utilization.

How the Principle Can Be Applied in the Classroom. Based on Principle #2, some instructional recommendations for teachers when implementing metacognitive assessments include the following.

- Encourage responses that illustrate exactly how a strategy is used by evaluating your word choice.
- Students sometimes respond based on what they think the teacher wants to hear, so teachers should request clarification or change assessment questions to ask students to identify when or where they demonstrate strategy.
- When choosing assessments, make sure they are associated with specific tasks.
- Administer assessments that students perceive to be of value to self-awareness of reading processes, and explain your rationale for using assessments.
- Anchor assessments to specific texts or reading tasks.
- Avoid questions that elicit hypothetical reactions such as, "What do you do when you get confused?"
- Ask students to compare and evaluate strategies they use before, during, and after reading.

Principle #3
Metacognitive assessments should be developmentally appropriate and sensitive to students' progressive reading knowledge and proficiency levels.

Assessment should be viewed as an important part of what drives your instructional interventions. Effective teachers choose assessments that are related to their instructional goals and understand that not all assessments are sensitive to a learner's needs. Therefore, it is necessary understand the developmental characteristics of students and differentiate instruction to meet the varying needs of all students. Before administering an assessment, ask yourself the following questions:

- What is my purpose for using this assessment?
- Do my students understand my rationale for giving this assessment?
- What information do I hope to obtain from this assessment and why?
- Will the assessment be completed within the allocated time limit?
- Am I sensitive to students' progressive proficiency knowledge?

Administering assessments that are developmentally appropriate can be a challenge for teachers who do not understand the developmental levels of their students. Likewise, as a result of developmentally inappropriate assessments students can feel frustrated, and their responses may not be valid. In addition, teachers should understand the proficiency levels of their students in order to set a baseline standard for instruction.

In a case study by Lowrie (1998), metacognitive strategies were integrated with the teaching of the strategy "taking another's point of view" during a gifted 6-year-old student's reading of the Goldilocks and the Three Bears story. A drawing activity and interview were used as mechanisms to move the student toward higher levels of metacognitive thought and to understand the child's thinking and perspective. This case study is relevant to teachers for several reasons. First, in this case the utilization of strategies reflected instructional goals as well as the combination of a few strategies being taught at the same time. Taking on someone else's point of view requires the student to activate higher order thinking strategies such as prediction, activating prior knowledge, summarizing, and reflecting strategies. Second, the metacognitive assessment was adapted for the child's age and ability level while at the same time not compromising the assessment goal of obtaining information about the child's reading abilities. Lastly, the metacognitive assessment utilized was repeated during different times throughout the reading of the story. What teachers can learn from this case study is that metacognitive assessments can be modified to specific individual needs.

Necessary Background Information. Based on this principle, it is important for teachers to possess an understanding of the following key ideas before administering metacognitive assessments.

- Students exhibit greater control and knowledge of strategies with age.

- Younger students might not be ready to verbalize their thoughts if they do not have prior knowledge of this concept.

- Older students have a broader range of reading experiences and are, therefore, more capable of providing more detailed information about thought processes.

How the Principle Can Be Applied in the Classroom. Based on Principle #3, some instructional recommendations for teachers when implementing metacognitive assessments include the following.

- Use assessments that involve gathering information to obtain accuracy, frequency, or effectiveness of specific strategies.

- Use language the students are able to understand in assessment measures.

- Understand purpose for using metacognitive assessments and communicate this to the students.

- With each assessment administered, make sure you have documented purpose for use and how results might influence specific aspects of reading.

- Develop habits of selecting or creating assessments when beginning a lesson or unit of study rather than at the end.

- If students are apprehensive about an assessment try to understand the child's reasoning or inquire about behaviors.

Principle #4

Metacognitive assessments should be used to complement existing measures of assessing reading fluency and comprehension.

You need not abandon the use of formal or informal assessments that are already in place in order to incorporate metacognitive assessments into your instruction. Metacognitive assessments can be integrated with existing measures with the understanding that they are used as the best form of measurement tool to obtain information about students' reading behaviors. In other words, metacognitive assessments should complement existing measures, not replace them. This does not mean that you need to add more assessments and possibly overwhelm your students (and yourself). You should identify the best measures available to help identify students' abilities in a specific area. Therefore, when selecting metacognitive assessments, ask yourself the following questions:

- Is this assessment developmentally appropriate?

- Does this assessment complement the comprehension assessments I am currently using?
- Are there certain measures I should not administer because the data do not support instructional goals? If so, which assessments?
- Is this assessment going to benefit my students, or will the data just be placed in file for documentation purposes?

By asking yourself these questions, you can ensure that your selections for assessments are based on the overarching instructional goals.

It is also important to use assessments consistently. In a study by Dewitz, Carr, and Patberg (1987), fifth-grade students with varying reading abilities were placed into one of three groups: high, middle, and low. Researchers in this study found that students with inference training using the cloze procedure that also integrated prior knowledge with text information had superior gains than that of the other treatment groups who did not receive this training. The metacognitive assessment used at the beginning and end of the study was a metacognitive interview, which included questions about the strategies being taught in the treatment groups. Dewitz and colleagues (1987) report, "In the final interview question, the students were asked to describe the strategies they would use to answer comprehension questions" (p. 118). What teachers can learn from this study is to use the same type of metacognitive assessment at the beginning and end of instruction so that the level of instructional gains can be measured consistently.

Necessary Background Information. Based on this principle, it is important for teachers to possess an understanding of the following key ideas before administering metacognitive assessments.

- Assessments can evaluate multiple aspects of reading processes.
- Students may have feelings of being overwhelmed with assessments, so take this into consideration. (If you are overwhelmed there is a good chance that students are, too.)

How the Principle Can Be Applied in the Classroom. Based on Principle #4, some instructional recommendations for teachers when implementing metacognitive assessments include the following.

- Choose assessments that are easy to administer and that can be combined with other assessments during reading.
- Use metacognitive assessments to understand strategy utilization and reading behaviors across multiple text types and reading tasks.

- Include think-alouds, interviews, or surveys to unit tests or content area reading to add value.
- Carefully evaluate assessments being used and consider adding on metacognitive assessments later.
- Do not add on assessments without telling students what you are doing.
- When assessing constructs like fluency or comprehension, add interview questions to assess strategy utilization.
- Add assessments to unit tests by asking students to evaluate strategic awareness during the unit.

Principle #5

Metacognitive assessments should be aligned with instructional goals so they provide diagnostic information about specific reading strategies.

Using assessments as diagnostic tools is way effective teachers gather information related to instructional goals and design effective intervention methods for students. Different assessments can be used with different types of students to obtain the greatest diagnostic evidence of each student's reading abilities.

The following items related to metacognitive assessments demonstrate how to align assessments with instructional goals:

- Identify curriculum to teach prior to beginning instruction.
- Decide the best form of assessments to use before, during, and after instruction.
- Value students' opinions about assessments, and strive to listen to and respect their opinions.
- Use assessment results to evaluate instructional goals.
- Once mastery level is achieved by some students, provide enrichment.

Effective teachers should not feel overwhelmed with assessments because they are using assessments that are appropriate for students and the information they want to obtain.

Palincsar and Ransom (1988) used metacognitive assessments to guide instruction and encourage teachers to become informed about strategic behaviors and metacognitive knowledge. One metacognitive assessment they used during literacy instruction is the think-aloud procedure (discussed in chapter 5 of this book). Palincsar and Ransom had students tutor each other, and during the tutoring session, the teacher noted directions the student gave, the hints suggested about the reading, and if the student made recommendations for improved reading. This information provided teachers with a window of what strategies the tutor viewed to be important as part of the reading task. What teachers can learn from this research is that "children's successes with learning is, in part, a function of their metacognitive knowledge and strategy use" (p. 786).

Necessary Background Information. Based on this principle, it is important for teachers to possess an understanding of the following key ideas before administering metacognitive assessments.

- Assessments should generate information that is integrated into daily instruction and yield immediate results that meet instructional goals.
- Teacher-created assessments are preferred over externally created measures.
- Assessments should be written in a manner that students can understand.
- It is essential to understand how to use diagnostic assessments to improve instruction.
- It is necessary to know instructional goals prior to selecting assessments.
- Assessment goals should be directly related to individual instructional needs.

How the Principle Can Be Applied in the Classroom. Based on Principle #5, some instructional recommendations for teachers when implementing metacognitive assessments include the following.

- Control how and when assessments are given during instruction.
- Use diagnostics to guide developmentally appropriate instruction for individual students.
- Teach metacogntive strategies that help students (especially poor readers) take control of the reading process.

Beliefs About Metacognitive-Oriented Reading Instruction

Before considering how to implement metacognitive assessments in your classroom, it is helpful to understand your current instructional beliefs on metacognition. An easy-to-use metacognitive self-assessment chart to help you reflect on your prior experiences and current conceptions about reading comprehension can be found on page 87 in Appendix A. Score yourself based on 1 = SD (Strongly Disagree) through 5 = SA (Strongly Agree), and use this information as a starting point in identifying areas in need of development or clarification.

What did you learn about yourself after reflecting on each statement? What do you want to gain from reading this book? Do you believe students should be more self-regulated readers in your classroom? What changes do you need to make in your instruction to develop metacognitively skilled readers? What puzzled you about your thinking on metacognitive assessments? Does your prior experience using informal or formal assessments affect your beliefs about the benefits of using metacognitive assessments?

CLASSROOM SCENARIO: Available Resources

You have more than 30 students in your classroom with no breaks during the day because your school cannot afford salaries for special area teachers. You know that analyzing assessment data takes time. Based on what you know about the principles of assessment, what metacognitive assessment will you administer? What is your rationale for doing so? The first thing you should do is make a list of assessments you are currently using and the instructional goals related to the reason to use assessment.

To help you understand how assessments are being used in your classroom you can refer to the sample Evaluation of Assessment Utilization in the Classroom chart in Figure 2. Follow this example to think critically about the benefits of assessment utilization and make decisions about which assessments should be used or deleted from the current repertoire of assessments being used.

Conclusion

The purpose of this chapter was to help you gain a solid understanding of the purposes, benefits, and research base for using metacognitive assessments and to discuss how integrating metacognitive assessments in the classroom will enable teachers to develop more effective instruction for individual students. You have learned about the five principles that will guide metacognitive assessments and the importance of these principles when planning how you will incorporate metacognitive assessments into your classroom practice. Chapter 2 will show you how to put this knowledge into action by explaining how to get started with using metacognitive assessments by using goal-setting strategies and activities to get students familiar with thinking metacognitively.

Resources to Enrich Your Understanding

Differentiated Assessment Strategies: One Tool Doesn't Fit All by Carolyn Chapman and Rita King (2005) is an excellent tool on learning how to use differentiated

Figure 2. Evaluation of Assessment Utilization in the Classroom

Assessments Currently Being Used	Instructional Goal	Decision to Continue to Use
QRI-4	To obtain information about reading comprehension fluency	Now, I am teaching first grade. None of my students can read. This assessment was more appropriate for me when I was teaching fifth grade last year. Although I feel comfortable with the procedures, I need to delete this assessment. Instead, I will add a reading inventory to administer in small groups.
Names Test by Cunningham	To obtain information about specific phonics strengths and weaknesses	This assessment was recommended to me by a second-grade teacher. However, my students still cannot read; therefore, I will not use this assessment with my first-grade students as I did last year. At this time of the school year, I will invite students to make a list of all the words they know and can spell in order to identify phonics ability. I will also ask them to explain to me what strategies they think they can use really well and can explain.

assessments in reading and content areas. The book offers a variety of assessment tools for various levels and learning styles. Another assessment resource I found useful in the classroom is a picture book called *Testing Miss Malarkey* (Finchler, 2000). I have used this book with fourth graders to get them to think differently about testing with the goal of reducing test anxiety. Two new professional books on reading assessments that I have used in my reading courses are *Children's Reading Comprehension and Assessment* (Paris & Stahl, 2005) and *Early Reading Assessment: A Practitioner's Handbook* (Rathvon, 2005). Paris and Stahl (2005) overview comprehension and metacognitive assessments in their research-based volume.

CHAPTER 2

Using Goal-Setting Activities as an Introduction to Metacognitive Assessments

---

CHAPTER GOALS

- Understand how goal setting can be used as a method to get students thinking metacognitively.
- Make connections with goal setting and metacognitive assessments as tools to guide individualized instruction.
- Understand how goal setting will aid in meaningful and productive outcomes for teachers and students.

In one of the senior-level reading courses for preservice teachers I once taught, I presented an overview of the theories related to metacognitive instruction. After reviewing various types of metacognitive thinking assessments and strategies, one of the preservice teachers asked me some very logical questions: "Where do I begin? How do I get started with using metacognitive assessments with my students? Do I just do everything?" This preservice teacher was being honest about how the students in her classrooms might be overwhelmed with the task of thinking metacognitively and about how she might be overwhelmed with the task of teaching her students to think metacognitively. In response to these questions, I suggested that this preservice teacher get started by helping her students set goals, and evaluate those goals based on achievement outcomes. My response made the preservice teacher feel more confident about implementing metacognitive practices as starting out with goal setting was an achievable objective from a teaching perspective, and this approach proved effective for her. Similarly, you may also find goal setting to be an effective starting point for getting your students to think metacognitively and for using metacognitive assessments in your classroom.

The purpose of this chapter is to explain the importance of goal setting and to help you use goals as a way to assess achievement with students. First you will learn how goal setting can be used as a precursor to metacognitive thinking and reading, a way to stimulate students' metacognitive abilities. Then, helpful goal-setting activities are provided, as well as additional activities to use as a way to introduce metacognitive thinking and assessments to students.

Goal Setting as a Precursor to Metacognitive Thinking and Reading

Schunk (2000) defines *goal* as something that reflects one's purpose and performance. He explains that goal setting has the process of establishing a standard or objective to serve as the aim of one's actions (p. 100) and that setting obtainable short-term goals leads to success at obtaining long-term goals. Goal setting is a behavior that is purposive and works toward a meaningful outcome. Commitment also plays a role in goal attainment. Behaviors done with commitment or conviction toward reaching a reasonable goal are more likely to be obtained.

From an early age children develop intrinsic motivation to achieve their goals. For example, do you remember learning how to tie your shoes and how proud you felt once you achieved this goal? One of my early academic goals was set in kindergarten, when I was determined to teach myself how to read; the desire to impress my teacher and make my parents proud of me motivated me to achieve this goal.

So how can goal setting be used to help students develop metacognitive thinking and reading? Students can be taught to activate their metacognitive thinking simply by learning how to set attainable goals, as goal setting of any kind inherently promotes metacognitive thinking and enhances students' ability to evaluate their own behaviors as they monitor their progress toward goal attainment. In other words, they are thinking about their own thinking as related to goal attainment. Therefore, when students think about their goals prior to reading they have a purpose for reading. Students are more likely to think critically about reading something that has a purpose in their lives as opposed to simply being told, "Read this." Teachers can use goal setting indirectly prior to reading by asking students at any age the questions What is your purpose for reading this text? What do you hope to gain when you are done reading? What is your overall reading goal, and how does this book help you attain that goal? When these questions are asked, students have something to think about, and this is when metacognitive thinking occurs. They can plan their reading goals by setting a purpose, they can monitor their reading goals while reading to see if the purpose is being met, and when they are finished they can evaluate their reading goals.

Samuels, Ediger, Willcut, and Palumbo (2005) support goal setting as a method to enhance development of metacognitive thinking during reading:

> Metacognitive instruction in the classroom begins with setting good attainable goals. Before a person starts to read, there are strategies that should be implemented to make a task more successful. For example, beginning readers are not aware of structure and organization of a book. In a classroom, teachers often read stories to emerging readers. However, in addition to reading to students, it is also helpful to have some discussion regarding why a student might want to read a particular text—that is, the teacher can help the learner establish a clear goal. (p. 53)

CLASSROOM SCENARIO: Communicating Assessment Goals

You are starting a new semester, and you plan to use metacognitive assessments to understand what students are thinking about reading instruction. As you present your students with these assessments, remember that assessment goals should always be explained and that explaining your own goals for the assessments is just as important as the need for students to identify their literacy goals. After assessments, it is equally important to review students' responses and provide feedback based on your assessment and instructional goals. Students can set personal goals based on your feedback. As time passes and assignments that help mastery of literacy goals are completed, new assessments can be administered. The process of assessment should be ongoing and reciprocal.

Using Goal Setting to Set the Stage for Metacognitive Assessments

Because goal setting aids in stimulating and increasing metacognitive thinking with students, it is a good idea to provide students with goal-setting experiences before using metacognitive assessments so that students can begin to develop self-evaluation and self-awareness strategies before they are asked to demonstrate their utilization of these types of strategies. I have found that it is not wise to assume that students intrinsically have the metacognitive ability to respond to questions in a reflective manner, complete survey items related to their awareness of reading behaviors or performance, and verbalize their thoughts if they are unsure what thoughts to verbalize. In my experience, it was important to scaffold students' ability to be reflective about their behaviors, and goal setting helped me do this because it was familiar ground to them.

At first, I made the assumption that I could give students a self-assessment on reading behaviors and they would be able to answer all the questions. What I discovered was that not everyone could think critically about their behaviors because they simply lacked experience with this way of thinking. When the students answered my questions with statements like "I don't know" or "I am not sure how to explain that," I realized that it was necessary to build their prior knowledge—as well as their confidence—about their ability to think in a reflective manner. Thinking metacognitively was a new concept and sometimes difficult for students, and by working with students on thinking metacognitively before administering the assessments I was able to achieve more accurate results that would better inform my instruction.

The research summarized by Schunk (2000) outlines several important aspects of goal setting that teachers need to be aware of when using goal setting with students to develop increased levels of metacognitive thinking prior to administering metacognitive assessments. These aspects are as follows:

- Goals need to be developmentally achievable.
- Modeling can increase students' ability to achieve their goals.
- Students who are motivated will exert more motivation to achieve their goals.
- Goals provide a pathway to a perceived and desired outcome.
- Goals help students stay focused.
- Evaluation of goal progress is important at all times.
- Goals should be divided into a series of achievable short-term to longer-term tasks.
- Goals should be "just right": not too hard and not too easy. (pp. 101–105)

According to Samuels and colleagues (2005), there are other functions that teachers can attend to when helping students learn about goal setting. During read-aloud experiences, teachers can help students become skilled in goal setting by asking a question such as, Why would you want to read this text? Teachers can also invite students to share their individual goals for reading or listening to a particular text. In addition, teachers should also explain to the students why they have selected a particular text for reading aloud. Finally, teachers can help students learn about the goals related to setting a purpose for their reading and have them ask themselves the following questions during a reading experience:

- Does what I am reading relate to my goal or purpose, and if so, how?
- How is what I just read related to this new information I am reading?
- How does the title of the book or subtitle in a section relate to my prior knowledge?

CLASSROOM SCENARIO: Goal Setting as a Strategy

You are beginning a new unit, and students are feeling confused about the assignment. Everyone in the class is asking you many questions. If you notice your students asking many questions about an assignment, they probably do not understand your expectations. Therefore, before students begin asking questions about the assignment, have them make a list of the goals they want to achieve. Compiling the information students provide, create a class goals sheet for the required assignment. Using student-generated goals helps reinforce self-regulation, and in this way, students' questions can be answered indirectly through a discussion session about the goals. If students still have questions, place students into small groups in order for them to help each other clarify information. Group members can then pick one student to ask any remaining questions about issues that need clarification.

Goal-Setting Activities

A good way to begin goal setting with students is to simply ask them to make a Personal To-Do List (see page 88 in Appendix A). First, explain to students how you use to-do lists to keep yourself organized. Then, enlarge the Personal To-Do List or create your own. Place the Personal To-Do List on the chalkboard or overhead, making sure all students can see the example, and have students complete the form first thing in the morning and review it at the end of each day prior to going home. You might also want to post your own Personal To-Do List for the class and model for students your thinking related to how you prioritize your tasks. Creating a Personal To-Do List serves as a precursor to metacognitive strategy instruction and assessments, as the list helps students to evaluate tasks—students activate monitoring strategies as they check off the tasks completed.

In the section that follows, several additional activities that you can use with your students to help them set literacy goals are provided.

Objective

The goal of this activity is to help students begin to generalize metacognitive mechanisms to aid in developing goal-setting strategies that are not particular to any task but useful across many (Crowley, Shrager, & Siegler, 1997).

Activating Prior Knowledge

Before beginning this lesson, students should have an understanding of goals and the reasons people set goals. For example, have students discuss the goals involved in a simple playground game, such as Four Square. Students can discuss the location and size of the squares and consider other important things about playing this game, such as having enough space around the four squares so they can catch the ball if it bounces to high or too far, and how these ideas are related to the object of the game.

Instructions

1. First, explain to students that goal setting is like working backward, similar to retracing one's steps to find a lost item or finding one's way out of a maze. Students can then relate this strategy to reading and looking at the end of the chapter or book to get a basic understanding of its content or looking at the review questions before reading.

2. Make copies of the maze found on page 89 in Appendix A.

3. Begin this activity by having students figure out the best way to get through a maze. Students should learn that working backward is the best way. Another alternative is to have students create their own mazes using chalk outdoors. Students can take turns working through their mazes.

4. Once students understand that working backward is most effective, begin to transfer this concept to reading tasks and comprehension of material. Ask students to decide what is the best way to get the general meaning of a book, or have students respond to review questions. If necessary, pair students who understand the concept of working backward with other students who are struggling with this concept.

Adaptations

1. Ask students to give examples of experiences they had when working backward helped them achieve a goal. Have students record their experiences in their journals to remind them of thinking backward to set goals.

2. Invite students to bring in maze books or activity books from home to share with other students, as many students enjoy maze or labyrinth games.

Objective

The goal of this lesson is to help students become metacognitively aware of their thoughts on a specific topic prior to any literacy activity. Students will be able to reflect on their thoughts related to prior knowledge of the topic, decide what procedures they need to take in order to understand the topic, and make decisions about how they will execute the procedures (Flavell, 1979).

Activating Prior Knowledge

Before beginning this lesson, tell students exactly what you are thinking about the literacy topic and what makes you think this way. Explain to them the procedures you might take in order to understand the topic and what actions you would take to obtain the information needed.

It is helpful for students if teachers introduce metacognitive terms and phrases in a sensitive manner. For example, when introducing metacognitive strategies and assessments, especially in the primary grades, provide further information and ensure that students understand terms like *plan*, *monitor*, and *evaluate* prior to beginning this task. Primary-grade teachers might want to work with the students to create visual aids or icons to represent these terms. For example, when I asked a third-grade student I was working with on comprehension strategies to create an icon for the word *think*, I was quite impressed with the icon she chose to use: It was a picture of thought bubble like the one in cartoon pictures. Because the student was the one who created this icon, she was able to remember this term and take ownership for its meaning.

Instructions

1. Using the reproducible What Am I Thinking? form on page 90 in Appendix A, ask students to write down all of their thoughts related to the literacy topic in the space inside the light bulb.

2. Using an overhead projection of the What Am I Thinking? form, complete the form with the students. Ask them what knowledge they have related to the topic and what knowledge they hope to gain from learning about the topic. Record this information in the "Knowledge" icon. In the "Procedural" icon, ask

students to tell them what procedures they need to take to obtain this knowledge. In the "Executive" icon, record how student will execute the literacy task.

3. Use the form you completed together at the end of the activity as an informal assessment tool to review students' thoughts on the literacy topic.

Adaptation

This form can be used with English-language learners (ELLs) and their parents to improve literacy communication. With students who are struggling to speak English, send the form home and invite parents to complete the form by translating their child's thoughts for them. Invite students to share other books they have read on the literacy topic, and have them explain their personal connections with the topic.

METACOGNITIVE MIND MAP

Objective

The Metacognitive Mind Map is a graphic organizer that aids students in making metacognitive connections between the text they are reading and other sources of information, familiar events, or experiences in their own life, and in making connections with world issues or events (see page 91 in Appendix A for a Metacognitive Mind Map tailored to primary-grade students, and see page 92 in Appendix A for a Metacognitive Mind Map tailored to students in the upper elementary grades).

Activating Prior Knowledge

Prior to beginning this lesson, discuss with students what you mean by making connections with other sources of information, personal experiences, and world issues or events. Give them an example of something you are reading and how you make similar text-to-text, text-to-self, and text-to-world connections (Keene & Zimmermann, 1997).

Instructions

1. Prior to discussing a topic or book, have students write down any connections they might have with other books, personal experiences, or world issues or events.

2. Using an overhead projector, share with the class the Metacognitive Mind Map, discuss these connections as a whole class and have students share responses they recorded.

3. Use the responses as a way to begin a discussion on the book or topic that the class will be reading or learning more about.

Adaptations

1. Because all learners have individual needs, have students choose one of their favorite ways to make connections.

2. When beginning a group project, have the entire group complete one Metacognitive Mind Map together. Instead of discussing the responses in a whole-group setting, have small groups meet with another small group.

GOLD RIBBON GOALS

Objective

The Gold Ribbon Goals activity is an informal metacognitive assessment that can be applied to any reading task. It helps students monitor their awareness and evaluate their progress when working to achieve their goals.

Activating Prior Knowledge

Prior to this lesson, have students write down their instructional goals they have set in the past, and have them brainstorm about how they went about attaining these goals.

Instructions

1. At the beginning of the school year or any time a new project begins, have students set individual literacy goals. Based on these goals, teachers can determine the type of assessment they believe will aid the students in their progress toward those identified goals. Using the reproducible Gold Ribbon Goals form found on page 93 in Appendix A, have students write down two or three important goals they would like to achieve for the literacy task.

2. Group students who have similar goals together and have them discuss how they can work together to achieve the goals. Invite students to brainstorm positive actions they can take when they have difficulty achieving their goals.

3. As the teacher, identify your own instructional goals and the assessments you want to administer to obtain rich data that supports instructional goals.

Adaptations

1. When students are working on small-group projects together, use the Gold Ribbon Goals activity to jump-start a conversation about instruction and learning.

2. Using a yellow highlighter, have students highlight one goal they would like help on and one assessment they need explained in more detail.

Additional Activities to Get Your Students Started With Metacognitive Thinking

To further help your students begin to develop their use of metacognitive thinking strategies, the following three activities can be easily applied or adapted in any literacy situation. Keeping My Mind on Reading is an activity that helps students pay attention to the reading task at hand. Metacognitive Sentence-by-Sentence Self-Monitoring for Small Groups will help scaffold students' metacognitive thinking and help students understand that thinking metacognitively is not something that happens once or twice while reading but something that happens naturally and throughout the reading process. Finally, the PBI Pyramid activity helps develop and increase students' higher order thinking skills and can be applied not only to reading but also to the content areas.

KEEPING MY MIND ON READING

Activity Goal

The goal of this activity is to help students monitor their understanding about what they are reading. The rationale for using this strategy is to help students begin to develop strategies that enable them to think independently. The images in the Keeping My Mind on Reading Street Signs sheet found on page 94 in Appendix A are meant to correspond with this activity and are especially helpful for students who are visual learners.

Activating Prior Knowledge

It would be helpful for students to understand what the word *monitor* means. You can provide students with the definition provided in the 11th edition of the Merriam-Webster's dictionary, which states that *monitor* means to watch or keep track of, or check for a special purpose.

Instructions

1. To help students monitor their comprehension of what they are reading and to help you easily identify students who are having difficult comprehending, have students place the three street signs on their desk. Before beginning have students color the signs as follows:

- Smiley face: green
- Caution sign: yellow
- Stop sign: red

Tell students to have the green sign with the smiley face on their desk when they understand what they are reading.

2. Have students use the yellow caution sign when they become slightly confused about the information in the text. When the yellow sign is being used, students can stop to ask a classmate a question about the text in order to try to get back on track with their understanding of the text.

3. When students have attempted to understand the text, but are still having difficulty, have them place the red stop sign on their desk, and permit them time to ask for clarification as needed.

Adaptations

1. Have students hold up a street signs that signal their level of understanding during a class discussion to check for understanding.

2. During paired reading, students who are reading together can use the street signs to signal their level of comprehension to their partner. At any given time, if students become confused about what they are reading, the street signs can be displayed.

3. You can change the meaning of the signs based on students' age or reading ability.

METACOGNITIVE SENTENCE-BY-SENTENCE SELF-MONITORING FOR SMALL GROUPS

Lesson Goal

Students will be able to attend to graphophonic and meaning cues in a sentence. The rationale for implementing this lesson is supported by research from Buettner (2002), who found increased levels of reading comprehension when more students did self-monitoring of their comprehension.

Activating Prior Knowledge

Make students aware that it is acceptable to ask for help. Discuss past situations when students asked for help, and it was beneficial to them. You should explain all the procedures and the rationale for the approach to reading practice. Students should have a functional knowledge of a sentence unit.

Instructions

1. Select a text appropriate for the grade level of your class.

2. Inform students that they will take turns reading a sentence. In the primary grades, you may want to have students practice their sentence in advance by themselves.

3. Activate the students' relevant background knowledge and direct them to make some predictions of what they might learn from the text.

4. Consider highlighting or numbering sentences for students when using the same text to facilitate smooth transitions.

5. Establish the expectation that all students will remain involved.

6. When one student is reading his or her sentence, the others should be silently reading the same sentence. You can assign roles to help with the record keeping and group facilitation.

7. While the student is reading the sentence, note any miscues. When students need support during reading or comprehension, prompt students to find the answers through their own thinking and reread sentences together, as the role of the teacher is mediator or coach. The following are suggested prompts, and after each prompt you should ask a "why" question to emphasize internalization and cognitive development.

   • Does this make sense?

   • Is that what we see in the picture?

   • Do you remember what happened to the...?

   • You read [repeat what student read]; the text is [repeat what is in the text]. Can you locate the part of the text that is inconsistent with what you read?

   • What part did you forget to look at?

   • Did the word you read make sense?

   • Can you reread the sentence correctly?

   • What word could you try to help you make sense?

   • What do you know that would help you?

8. To complete the activity, ensure that cohesive sentence integration has occurred by keeping accurate records during this small-group work (see the reproducible Metacognitive Sentence-by-Sentence Self-Monitoring Record on page 95 in Appendix A). Strive for the goal of moving from small-group instruction on this skill to student independence.

Adaptations

1. Practice using student-selected materials. The same approach can be modified for student writing samples.

2. Use one or more of the following activities to help with sentence integration:

   • Mix up sentence strips and have students place them in correct order.

   • Have students draw pictures for each sentence to depict their understanding.

   • Have students act out each sentence.

   • Have each student select another sentence that was read, and use the two sentences to create a new sentence or story.

   • Ask each group to identify their favorite sentence and have them relate what they learned in the sentence to something in their own life, another book that they read, or something going on in the world.

PBI PYRAMIDS

Lesson Goal

The goal of using PBI (Process-Based Instruction) Pyramids is to help students increase planning processes through a series of phases (Ashman, Wright, & Conway, 1994).

Activating Prior Knowledge

Discuss with the class their previous experiences with problem-solving strategies, such as those utilized when reading stories where the main character has to solve a problem (e.g., books in the Harry Potter series).

Instructions

1. Prior to beginning the PBI Pyramid planning activity, have a class discussion in which you relate plans and planning to students' own experiences (e.g., stories about household routines or stories about how teams go about breaking through the defense of the opposing team).

2. Familiarize students with the PBI process, and make them aware of how plans can assist them in learning. Explain the following four phases of the planning pyramid model:

   • The Introduction Phase: Students becomes familiar with the task and begin to outline a plan of action to complete the task. Where and how do I start?

- The Establishment Phase: Students analyze the plan for completing another task in order to develop an understanding of the relationship of the plan to other tasks. What is the sequence of actions?
- The Consolidation Phase: Students make decisions about what actions or decisions are needed in order to deal with new situations in a different context. Students learn how to draw on experiences to guide behavior. Is the plan effective?
- The Incorporation Phase: Students learn how to develop and transfer plans to new situations in which general plans are necessary. Has the task been completed successfully?

3. Using the reproducible PBI Pyramid provided on page 96 in Appendix A, begin by helping smaller groups work together to prepare steps in planning actions to solve a problem or task.

Adaptation

Use the PBI Pyramid as an evaluation tool and have students evaluate their understanding.

Conclusion

In this chapter you have learned how you can get students started with metacognitive thinking by using goal-setting strategies. Several goal-setting activities have been included in this chapter to help students get started with thinking metacognitively—and to help you begin thinking about how to start using metacognitive assessments to create individualized literacy instruction for your students.

The next three chapters will discuss three types of research-supported metacognitive assessments. Chapter 3 provides the reader with many examples of how to use interviews to obtain information on metacognitive strategy utilization. Chapter 4 explains different ways to integrate inventories and surveys in all areas of literacy and with existing assessment tools to obtain effective diagnostic data. Chapter 5 provides the reader with many examples on how to use think-alouds as an assessment tool. After reading the next three chapters on metacognitive assessments, you can return to goal setting and use this knowledge when developing individualized instruction.

A valuable resource for reflecting on practice in order to set goals that will aid in developing metacognitively skilled readers is *Motivating Primary-Grade Students* (Pressley et al., 2003). This is a wonderful research-based resource on motivation that helps teachers reflect on actions that motivate and undermine student motivation. I use this book when I teach preservice middle school teachers as an assessment tool for self-discovery on strategies to increase student motivation. When I use goal setting as a tool to motivate my students, I use self-assessments as a way to understand what they like best. A picture book I use with my students when I want them to think about what they like is *I'm Gonna Like Me: Letting Off a Little Self-Esteem* by Jamie Lee Curtis and Laura Cornell (2002).

CHAPTER 3

Interviews as Metacognitive Assessment Tools

The interview approach is familiar to students of all ages and certainly one that teachers have used in the past for many instructional purposes. Interviews are usually administered in a one-on-one setting and are particularly effective for obtaining data about students' metacognitive processes. This chapter focuses on the administration and analysis of interviews that are designed to obtain detailed information about students' metacognitive beliefs about reading behaviors. Interviews can also be used to evaluate levels of strategic knowledge immediately following direct instruction or intervention. The information gathered during an interview is used to enhance literacy learning at the individual level. Therefore, the interview methods described in this chapter are to be used in individual interviews with students.

Rationale for Using Metacognitive Interviews

Interviews are known to be valid and reliable sources of information, and it is recommended that teachers use them to understand metacognitive awareness (Pressley & Afflerbach, 1995). So why *should* teachers use interviews as metacognitive assessments? One reason that interviews are so effective at determining students' metacognitive awareness is because teachers can take advantage of the open-ended format of interviews in order to obtain detailed information about each student's knowledge level of specific strategies and individual behaviors as related to the reading process. For example, interviews can be used to understand each student's specific awareness of reading behaviors and strategies used as part of the PME Framework (as discussed in the Introduction), such as what the student does prior to reading (planning), what is done when meaning construction is lacking (monitoring), and the learner's personal thoughts on what was read (evaluating). Content area teachers can use interviews to obtain knowledge about strategies that are difficult for students to apply when reading difficult nonfiction text.

In addition, because the administration of interviews is very informal, teachers have the opportunity to invite students to elaborate on their responses. Interviews should include open-ended type questions that are developmentally appropriate. Teachers can invite students to respond to general reading processes or about any specific experience during or after reading (Israel, Bauserman, et al. 2005; Paris & Flukes, 2005). Furthermore, questions used during an interview can be tailored to specific student needs. For example, students have the opportunity to ask for further explanations of words, concepts, or phrases that teachers otherwise may assume are common knowledge. Because the knowledge gained from interviews is so individualized to each student's needs and abilities, interviews are a highly effective type of metacognitive assessment for aiding teachers in creating reading instruction that is individualized.

CLASSROOM SCENARIO: Thinking Metacognitively

Do you think interviews should be organized around a specific literacy event? Interviews certainly can be organized around specific literacy events, like feelings about test taking or confidence levels about oral reading. However, interviews can also be used to obtain general information about students' cognitive and affective reading behaviors. Regardless of the event or circumstance, always consider developmental level, presentation of interview, and confidence level of students about the assessment task and goal.

Guidelines for Using Interviews as Metacognitive Assessments

Interviews can be conducted throughout the school year and before and after specific metacognitive strategy instruction. Keep in mind that when working with individual students to improve reading abilities, the key benefit of using interviews is that teachers can effectively obtain concrete information about students' awareness of reading behaviors on a more personal level as opposed to other metacognitive assessments, such as surveys (discussed in chapter 4). Therefore, teachers should personalize individual questions and give students an opportunity to ask questions or elaborate on answers.

Interviewing students about reading behaviors is a valuable method to obtain information about metacognitive awareness, but it is important to understand exactly what to look for during student interviews. There are specific research-based guidelines that should be followed when considering using the interview process as a metacognitive assessment tool. You can use the assessment guidelines in the following section when preparing for individual metacognitive interviews of strategic reading behaviors.

Attention to Learner-Centered Assessments

Teachers should write questions in language that students can understand (Block & Pressley, 2002; Pressley & Afflerbach, 1995). This means that teachers should use or write assessments using language that is clear, direct, and appropriate for age and grade level. In addition, if you have students who are English-language learners (ELLs), it would be highly beneficial to provide questions in the students' native language or provide students with a more able peer who can help with reading and understanding the questions and speak the native language. Parents can also be a resource for teachers by interpreting questions for their child so that the child can understand what is being asked. The ELL population has increased in schools, and teachers are faced with challenges on how to effectively reach ELL and English as a second language (ESL) students.

Expressing Explicit Goals

Interview questions should not be vague but should focus on specific types of reading strategies or processes a teacher is trying to understand (Block & Pressley, 2002; Paris & Flukes, 2005). Therefore, teachers should focus on questions that provide opportunities to help increase students' awareness of these specific strategies (Paris & Flukes, 2005). Also, it is important to explain specific aspects of the interview process and how you will use the information gained to evaluate literacy goals and to help the student in literacy learning.

Plan Assessment Connections

More than one assessment approach is recommended when it comes to understanding metacognitive awareness and literacy behaviors. Therefore, interviews can and should be used with other metacognitive assessments such as surveys and inventories (see chapter 4) or think-alouds (see chapter 5). In particular, the Index of Reading Awareness (Jacobs & Paris, 1987; see page 54 in this chapter for further discussion and pages 104–106 in Appendix B for the full assessment) is a multiple-choice assessment tool that correlates well with informal interviews and other metacognitive assessments. Although some of the questions might target identical behaviors, students have an opportunity to explain how they feel during an interview. Sometimes it is difficult for students to explain their responses when responding to scripted surveys and inventories (which is why it is good practice to use more than one assessment approach when evaluating students' reading behaviors), but students' are often able to more clearly express themselves during interviews. Teachers can use these responses and look for consistency in responses across all types of metacognitive assessments in order to identify areas of strengths and areas for improvement.

Metacognitive Interviews to Use in Your Classroom

In the following section, four examples of metacognitive interview formats that you can use anytime throughout the school year are discussed, though it is recommended that you use interview methods prior to beginning a school year, if possible. Interviews can be conducted effectively during a back-to-school night or when your school holds an open house. If teachers at your school schedule a meet-the-teacher day, this is also an excellent opportunity to conduct interviews with students.

Back-to-School Individual Meta-Interview

This interviewing format can be used as a diagnostic tool for understanding your students' existing reading behaviors—their reading behaviors before coming to your classroom. Invite students to attend a back-to-school student–teacher conference by sending them a postcard. You can use an invitation similar to the sample in Figure 3, which is very similar to the one I used at the beginning of every school year.

During the interview, have a table set up with the supplies you need and an interview form to take notes on, such as the Back-to-School Interview Form provided on page 97 in Appendix A. The questions in this interview form, of course, can be modified for specific grade levels. I found that color-coding my forms helped me keep organized, so I usually copied the form in a bright color. The interview form features five questions. I did not want to overwhelm students

CLASSROOM SCENARIO: Finding Time for Metacognitive Interviews

The students in your class require a lot of attention, and you do not know how to schedule additional time for student interviews. Finding time to conduct metacognitive interviews and other metacognitive assessments is a concern shared by many teachers, but there are many ways to make time for these important diagnostic tools. First, consider what you can do to rearrange your schedule or what your colleagues do in similar situations. If time still does not permit you to schedule individual conferences, then schedule small-group conferences with students of similar needs.

The following are some additional pointers for saving time.

- Think critically about your day to see if there are ways to conserve your time. Do you use your teacher prep times wisely? Do you find yourself having to repeat directions too frequently? How do you pass out papers in the classroom? Do you organize students before they go to special events and for what comes after?

- Evaluate the time not spent on instruction during a typical school day. Do you spend a lot of time organizing or looking for supplies? Do all your students have classroom jobs? Do you spend too much time waiting for students to get organized? Are there ways you can use some of this time more effectively?

- Include more parent volunteers to do seasonal classroom decorating and planning for activities (see Table 5 for more ideas on how to effectively employ parent volunteers for classroom activities in order to secure more time for you to conduct interviews and other metacognitive assessments).

- Minimize time spent standing in lines, such as group trips to the drinking fountains or bathrooms. Can you use a hall pass when sending students to the bathroom? Do you have long lines of students standing at your desk waiting to ask you a question? Are all the questions similar or can they be answered easily by a peer?

- Assign homework that is meaningful so that you have more free time and less grading. Does everything have to be graded? Are grades being used in assessment results related to achievement?

during the interview so I tried to ask only questions that would help me understand each student's metacognitive awareness. As an alternative to this interview form, primary-grade teachers might want to have students use crayons and pictures and fill in the Visual Back-to-School Interview Form found on page 98 in Appendix A. You can make two copies of the form, giving one to the student and keeping one copy on which to take notes on what the students says while drawing the pictures.

Other activities to motivate students during the back-to-school interviews (or even during interviews conducted throughout the school year) are as follows.

Figure 3. Sample Back-to-School Individual Meta-Interview Invitation

You are invited to a
Teacher–Student Back-To-School Conference

Dear 1st Grader,

Welcome to 1st Grade! I am so excited to be your teacher and I am looking forward to meeting you. Because I want to be a very good teacher, I would like to get to know your thoughts about reading and writing.

Where: Mrs. Israel's Classroom Room 110A
When: August 15, 2007, During Open House
Time: Sign up for a conference from 12:00 p.m.–3:00 p.m.

I am looking forward to an exciting school year!

Sincerely,

Mrs. Israel

Favorite Book Bag. Have students put together a bag of their favorite books and bring the bag to the interview. I recommend a variety of fiction, nonfiction, or print materials that the child reads. Be sure to inform students that they will need to prepare these items ahead of time in order to bring them to the conference (e.g., you may want to note this on their Back-to-School Individual Meta-Interview Invitation).

Autobio-Bags. Ask students to prepare a Literature Autobiography Bag (Weih, 2006) and bring the bag to the interview (again, you may want to note this request on the student's Back-to-School Individual Meta-Interview Invitation). Have students place bio-related objects that are significant to them and that they can talk about in a bag or box. Teachers can use the artifacts to interview students using some of the same questions outlined above.

Conference Collage. Have each student create a collage during the interview describing himself or herself as a reader, and attach a photo to the collage. You can hang the collage on the child's desk with his or her nametag. The visual will help prompt discussions with other students when school starts or remind you of the child.

Interview Tours. Invite your students to tour the literacy activities and resources in your classroom to help them feel comfortable in your learning environment. During the tour, conduct the interview by asking them questions to help you understand their metacognitive awareness.

Table 5. Ways to Effectively Use Parent Volunteers to Create More Teacher Time for Conducting Metacognitive Assessments

In order to secure more instructional time to devote to metacognitive interviews and other metacognitive assessments, have parent volunteers assist you with some of the following classroom activities:

- Laminating or binding classroom books
- Photocopying weekly assignments one day a week
- Cutting papers for special activities
- Hanging seasonal bulletin boards
- Researching specific items, such as planning field trips
- Gathering content materials for thematic units
- Coordinating book orders
- Making phone calls to schedule field trips, guest speakers, or special class activities
- Typing class newsletters with students
- Assisting in monitoring class movies
- Working with students in small-group activities once a week
- Donating class supplies so you do not have to take time to purchase them
- Making books or journals at home
- Walking students to special school activities or to the bus
- Monitoring or sitting with students during special school activities
- Gathering library books for your classroom
- Picking up community resources such as teacher kits from museums
- Mailing letters
- Developing classroom photos from field trips
- Doing read-alouds with students once a week

Peer Meta-Views

During the school year students spend a lot of time with their peers and in collaborative learning groups. A way to help students learn about effective metacognitive strategies that good readers use is to have children interview their classmates or peers. Using the same questions provided in the Back-to-School Interview Form and Visual Back-to-School Interview Form found in Appendix A, teach a group of students how to interview other students. Then begin with those students who have learned how to interview, and have them interview other classmates. The peer prompts in the Peer Meta-View Prompts form found on page 99 in Appendix A can be photocopied and used with students who will be conducting the peer meta-interviews. The classmates will begin modeling the interview process for the students who have not been trained, and more students, therefore, will eventually be trained to conduct interviews.

These Peer Meta-Views are often effective because some students might feel more comfortable talking with their peers as opposed to adults and because they are interested in gaining new knowledge about how others read. In grade levels where students are already comfortable with writing, students can write down what they learned in the interview or return to a teacher conference to report some of the findings.

Guided Interviews Using the Index of Reading Awareness

Jacobs and Paris's (1987) Index of Reading Awareness includes questions that specifically focus on understanding components of metacognition, such as planning strategies (see pages 104–106 in Appendix B for the full assessment). The responses are given a score of a (0) inappropriate response, (1) a partially adequate answer, and (2) strategic response. For example, the teacher might read the following question during the interview and ask the student to select the response that best describes him or her as a reader:

> Before you start to read, what kind of plans do you make to help you read better?
> a. You don't make any plans. You just start reading. (0)
> b. You choose a comfortable place. (1)
> c. You think about why you are reading. (2)

After the interview, the teacher can tally the scores and identify areas of reading strengths and make a list of suggestions for improvement.

Conclusion

In this chapter, you learned that interviews are metacognitive assessments that teachers can use in a one-on-one setting to obtain specific information about each student's utilization and awareness of reading behaviors. Interviews correlate with other metacognitive assessments and aid teachers in identifying strengths and areas for improvement. Interviews can be used with students of all ages and can be personalized to meet individual student needs. In the next chapter, you will learn about surveys and inventories and the benefits of using these types of metacognitive assessments to create individualized reading instruction.

A picture book that I recommend using with students, especially younger ones, to help them feel comfortable in interview situations is called *An Interview With Harry the Tarantula* by Leigh Ann Tyson (2003). The author used the interview technique to learn about the behaviors of the tarantula. This nonfiction picture book can be used prior to conducting an interview or read at the start as an interview model. Another book I recommend is a Newbery Award–winning book, *Criss Cross* by Lynne Rae Perkins (2005). One of the characters in the book, Lenny, enjoys reading nonfiction books like encyclopedias and shares his thoughts about the visual images that appear in his mind when reading: "He looked for a while at the drawings without making any mental effort. Then in his brain, the drawings converged briefly into a three-dimensional animated mode...." (p. 57). The book can be used as a read-aloud as a model to motivate older readers to share their thoughts.

In addition, a resource not from the area of literacy but from the area of business and leadership is helpful for conducting metacognitive interviews: a webpage on how to conduct professional interviews found at www.management help.org/evaluatn/intrview.htm. This webpage summarizes key strategies to get in-depth information. Interview tips include preparing for an interview (explain your rationale), open-ended and fixed-response interviews (ask the same questions and choose from a list of responses), wording of questions (avoid wording that influences answers), and what to do immediately after an interview (write down observations).

CHAPTER 4

Surveys and Inventories as Metacognitive Assessment Tools

CHAPTER GOALS
• Become familiar with how to use surveys and inventories by learning about administrative guidelines.
• Make informed decisions about metacognitive assessment utilization by reflecting on a variety of surveys and inventories.
• Learn how to differentiate surveys and inventories in order to enhance reading instruction for all learners.

This chapter explains how to use two types of metacognitive assessments: surveys and inventories. Surveys and inventories are similar to interviews in that both types of assessments inquire about reading behaviors and can be used to determine students' metacognitive strategy utilization. However, unlike interviews, surveys and inventories focus more on the assessment of targeted reading behaviors rather than open-ended inquiry questions, and responses are usually in the format of multiple-choice questions.

Many teachers may find surveys and inventories especially appealing because they are less time-consuming than other assessments, such as interviews. Surveys and inventories are also well suited for teachers who want to obtain information from the larger class population or groups rather than individuals, as surveys are designed to be used in large groups and to sample proficiencies in specific areas (Harris & Hodges, 1995), and inventories, while still appropriate for larger groups, are most effective when administered in small-group settings.

Rationale for Using Surveys and Inventories

What are the benefits of using surveys and inventories? Surveys and inventories, like interviews (see chapter 3), can be used to assess specific strategies related to planning, monitoring, and evaluating the reading processes. However, unlike interviews, which are conducted one-on-one with individual students, surveys and inventories are easy to use with an entire class or with groups of students in the class—the questionnaire format lends itself to usage with groups of any size, and because the questions have already been designed to assess targeted behaviors, less preparation is required. Teachers can explain the directions once for all the students and score or analyze the data much quicker than they can administer and obtain data through interviews, which require individual time with each student.

In addition, surveys and inventories give teachers an opportunity to understand their students in a way that demonstrates that they value and are attentive to their students' level of understanding about their own literacy behaviors. Surveys and inventories are also beneficial to teachers because they already offer explanations for assessment results, providing concrete information that teachers can use to support their understanding of their students' reading behaviors and therefore gauge how to go about meeting students' individual literacy needs.

Other benefits for using surveys and inventories as metacognitive assessments include the following:

- Using a variety of surveys and inventories allows teachers to gain knowledge about students' understanding about literacy development and their concerns and beliefs about reading.
- Surveys and inventories can be used in large- or small-group settings to obtain information about metacognitive proficiency levels.
- Teachers can still obtain individual profiles for students, yet surveys and inventories are less time-consuming for teachers to administer and score.
- Surveys and inventories provide a variety of question formats (e.g., multiple choice), which can lead to more reliable results.
- Surveys and inventories allow students to self-report reading behaviors.

Guidelines for Using Surveys and Inventories as Metacognitive Assessments

Before beginning strategy instruction, teachers should spend time assessing their own use of strategies (Block et al., 2002). Therefore, an important step to using and understanding metacognitive surveys and inventories would be to take the assessments discussed in this chapter yourself. Completing the assessments prior to using them in your classroom will help you decide which metacognitive assessments are most appropriate and will best fit your students' needs. It will also alert you to any vocabulary words that you might need to explain to students prior to administering the assessments.

Because surveys and inventories are easy to administer and evaluate, teachers can administer them more frequently, allowing students to have more opportunities to monitor their own level of understanding of strategy utilization and effectiveness. Therefore, teachers can use surveys and inventories as often as necessary for instructional purposes to monitor and evaluate students' awareness of reading processes (Afflerbach, 1996; Israel, 2002; Pressley & Afflerbach, 1995). Teachers can use metacognitive assessments as a way to evaluate and measure ongoing instruction related to metacognitive strategies and reading comprehension.

Teachers can also use the additional assessment guidelines in the following section when preparing for and administering metacognitive surveys and inventories of strategic reading behaviors.

Reinforce Assessment Goals

Surveys and inventories, like all metacognitive assessments, should reinforce assessment goals. Assessment goals would be related to teachers' individual instructional goals or overall classroom proficiency goals. For example, if your assessment goal as a teacher is to better understand what type of strategies students are familiar with prior to reading, using the Metacomprehension Strategy Index would be effective because the assessments evaluates strategies used before, during, and after reading (see page 65 in this chapter for more information on this inventory and pages 114–117 in Appendix B for the full inventory). Using this inventory will allow you to understand what students are doing before they read and what they need to know how to do before they read, allowing you to target specific strategies rather than teaching strategies already mastered.

Encourage Honesty

It is important to help students understand that when responding to open-ended questions, all of their responses or thoughts are important. Before I administer any survey or inventory, I tell my students, "Your thoughts are very important to me. Do not be afraid to let me know how you feel about...."

Critically Reflect on Student Responses

Teachers need to critically reflect on students' responses to make sure they mirror students' abilities and are not just random responses to the questions. Teachers should use their own judgment to determine whether a student's response reflects genuine understanding or is based on what he or she thinks the teacher wants to hear (Block et al., 2002; Duffy, 2003; Paris & Flukes, 2005; Pressley & Afflerbach, 1995).

Share Results

Discussing assessment results with students is very important. A mistake I made early on in my teaching career was administering assessments for personal use. Usually the assessments were placed in a file for future reference, perhaps during a parent conference. Later in my career, I realized that it is unfair for students who take time to complete an assessment not to know the results or how this information will benefit them in the literacy process.

Support Self-Monitoring

Students benefit from knowing their strengths related to metacognitive awareness as well as their areas for improvement. I believe all students want to be self-regulated, and therefore teachers should create opportunities for them to develop this level of understanding. Using surveys and inventories more than once and communicating results will provide concrete evidence for students on reading strategies they are doing really well or ones they need more practice with. In addition, simply reading and going through the questions and results will provide students with an awareness of what they can be doing to improve reading, giving them an opportunity to reflect critically and monitor their own reading behaviors. When students are given time to reflect on the results, they begin to develop metacognitive awareness; when students begin to achieve this awareness they may say things like "Oh, now I understand how to use this strategy" or "This is a new way to read, and using this strategy will also help me with comprehension."

Metacognitive Surveys and Inventories to Use in Your Classroom

The following section presents different types of surveys and inventories teachers can use in their classrooms to assess students' metacognitive abilities and strategy utilization.

Reading Strategy Awareness Inventory

The Reading Strategy Awareness Inventory (Miholic, 1994) is a metacognitive assessment that will help you identify difficulties that students may experience while reading such as the following:

- Understanding new words
- Recalling important information
- Knowing what to do before reading

This inventory offers a list of 10 questions that refer to three different types of metacognitive strategies: planning, monitoring, and evaluation (see pages 6–7 in the Introduction for further descriptions of these types of strategies). This assessment provides information about what happens in a student's mind regarding comprehension construction. This inventory can be adapted for different ages or learning styles by removing the choices and allowing students to answer the questions freely. You can also read the questions and the responses to the students.

Two versions of this form have been provided in Appendix B: the Reading Strategy Awareness Inventory (see pages 107–108), and an adapted Reading Strategy Awareness Inventory, Open-Ended Format (see page 109). The Reading Strategies Awareness Inventory offers specific responses students can select, while the Reading Strategies Awareness Inventory, Open-Ended Format asks the same questions but without responses to select. The adapted open-ended version of this inventory allows students to communicate their personal understanding or knowledge levels, and this format can also be used as a differentiated assessment format for students who struggle with reading, helping them feel more comfortable when responding.

When analyzing the results of this inventory, Miholic cautions teachers to take into consideration the reader and instruction. Teachers will find it helpful to make a list of the strategies the students used when analyzing the results of this inventory (see the Reading Strategy Awareness Inventory Analysis Form on page 100 in Appendix A and a sample analysis in Figure 4). Making a list will also help create a student profile of intervention strategies. To complete this analysis, use the second column to list the actual student responses to the questions included in the inventory and use the third column to list possible intervention strategies based on the student responses.

Metacognitive Awareness of Reading Strategies Inventory (MARSI)

The MARSI (Mokhtari & Reichard, 2002) is a self-report instrument with 10 questions designed to measure readers' metacognitive awareness (see pages 110–113 in Appendix B for the full assessment). Elementary teachers can benefit from using the MARSI to learn more about how students read academic or

Figure 4. Sample Analysis for Reading Strategy Awareness Inventory

Student: Mary (Grade 1)
Date: 9/15

Assessment Question	How a Student Might Respond	What to Suggest to Student for Improvement
1. What do you do if you encounter a word and you don't know what it means?	Ignores word (Items a, b, c)	Try to use words around it to figure it out
2. What do you do if you don't know what an entire sentence means?	Sounds out difficult words (Items a, c)	Think about other sentences in the paragraph
3. If you are reading science or social studies material, what would you do to remember the important information you've read?	Skips parts (Items b, c, d)	Try to relate it to prior knowledge
4. Before you start to read, what kind of plans do you make to help you read better?	Think about what I know (Items b, c)	Recall purpose for reading and predict how prior knowledge and new knowledge will respond to purpose
5. Why would you go back and read an entire passage over again?	Didn't understand (Items a, c, d)	Try to reread to look for important information
6. Knowing that you don't understand a particular sentence while reading involves understanding that...	Meaning in sentences slows down reading (Items a, b, c)	Think about how the sentences relate to one another
7. As you read the textbook, which of these do you do?	Skips confusing parts (Items a, d)	Try to use monitor strategies
8. While you read, which of these are important?	Know what it is that I already know and why this would be important (Items a, b, d)	Reinforce strategies of activating prior knowledge to build confidence in reading and comprehension
9. When you come across a part of the text that is confusing, what do you do?	Keep reading (Items a, b, d)	Encourage to stop reading and identify point when text was confusing and decide to look back for important ideas
10. Which sentences are most important in the chapter?	Ones with most detail (Items b, c)	Understanding what a main idea is and help locate sentences that directly relate to the main idea

Assessment questions from Miholic, V. (1994). An inventory to pique students' metacognitive awareness of reading strategies. *Journal of Reading, 38,* 84–86. Reprinted with permission from the International Reading Association and V. Miholic.

school-related materials. Three types of reading strategies are defined and analyzed: global, problem-solving, and support. The MARSI can be used to understand what students think about and what reading processes occur when they read academic or informational materials such as textbooks or library books.

Similar to the Reading Strategy Awareness Inventory (Miholic, 1994), this inventory also assesses awareness of specific strategies but focuses specifically on the metacognitive-oriented strategies that students utilize during reading and is based on the understanding that different strategies are used when reading different types of texts. In addition, this inventory offers a different format that teachers can select based on personal teaching goals.

This assessment also provides useful information in the scoring section, and teachers can learn what strategies students *should* be using when reading. For example, you can use this inventory to discover that a student is using global reading strategies—those strategies students use when analyzing an entire text—more than problem-solving strategies. According to the authors of the MARSI (Mokhartri & Reichard, 2002), global reading strategies—such as setting a purpose for reading or making predictions about content prior to reading—are more general and set the stage for the reading act.

The developers of the instrument (Mokharti & Reichard, 2002) report that the MARSI has demonstrated that results are reliable and a valid measure for assessing students' metacognitive awareness, specifically related to academic-type reading. This is particularly useful due to the fact that research has found that not all students are capable of transferring strategy utilization across text types.

While the MARSI is an excellent assessment tool for helping students to increase their awareness of metacognitive ability, teachers should not use the assessment to evaluate students' comprehension-monitoring abilities. When tailoring individual instruction for students, teachers can use the results in the following ways:

- To understand how students have evaluated their reading awareness
- To understand the types and numbers of reading strategies used by students
- To understand reading strategy utilization under different conditions (e.g., when reading fiction as opposed to nonfiction, academic reading as opposed to recreational reading)

The authors of this inventory recommend that teachers use the information gleaned from this assessment as a supplement to other assessment measures (which is consistent with the principles of metacognitive assessments discussed in chapter 1). Because the MARSI is used as a tool for students to self-report, teachers should be attentive to the fact that students may or may not actually utilize the strategies they report. When making instructional decisions, teachers will need to keep a sharp eye on their interpretations and keep students' needs and behaviors in mind.

Metacomprehension Strategy Index (MSI)

The MSI (Schmitt, 2005; see pages 114–117 in Appendix B) is a multiple-choice assessment tool with 25 questions that was developed as an instrument to understand student's level of comprehension awareness. The MSI measures strategies within the following six general areas:

1. Predicting
2. Previewing
3. Purpose setting
4. Self-questioning
5. Activating prior knowledge
6. Summarizing and applying fix-up strategies

The MSI can be used with students when teachers want to identify specific reading behaviors that occur before, during, and after reading. The questions are correlated with specific metacognitive strategies that allow students to plan, monitor, and evaluate reading comprehension.

The MSI was created to be used in larger group settings with students who can read fluently, but it can easily be used with teachers working in smaller groups or individually depending on reading levels of students. Because there are no right answers in the MSI, Schmitt recommends that teachers use the results of the index to consider what strategies students were already familiar with; the differences among before, during, and after reading; as well as any patterns that suggest difficulty in specific areas.

For younger students or students who have trouble responding to multiple-choice questions, a modified version of the MSI is provided (see the Metacognitive Strategies Inventory on page 118 in Appendix B).

Differentiated Analytic Reading Self-Assessment

The Differentiated Analytic Reading Self-Assessment (Afflerbach & Meuwissen, 2005) is a 12-item inventory divided into the following five categories:

1. Previewing the Text
2. Capturing the Text
3. Rereading the Text

4. Evaluating the Text

5. Responding to the Text

The inventory is written using statements that promote the development of self-assessment abilities and student learning of strategies within the English language arts curriculum for middle school students but can be used with all types of learners at most grade levels depending on reading ability. I created a modified version of this inventory for elementary students so that emerging readers can begin to think about strategies they use while reading or when others are reading with them (see the Differentiated Analytic Reading Self-Assessment, Adapted for Elementary Grades on page 119). This assessment is different from the MARSI and the MSI in that it is written so that students can reflect on their reading strategy utilization and awareness each time they read. I recommend you review the faces with students and what each face means. As primary students become more familiar with the behaviors they do well or behaviors that needs improvement, students draw their own face and explain what the face means to them. This assessment is particularly useful for English-language learners who need modified assessment formats and modifications on the statements.

Differentiating Metacognitive Surveys and Inventories

The surveys and inventories presented in this chapter provide excellent resources for learning about your students' metacognitive strategy awareness and capabilities, but some students may still need differentiated assessments based on learning styles or needs. The following section outlines approaches for differentiating metacognitive assessment surveys and inventories to better fit your needs and the needs of your students.

Differentiating Surveys and Inventories for Students Who Struggle With Reading

Students who struggle with reading may also struggle when responding to surveys or inventories about reading. Therefore, it is important to first help these students understand some of the common words found in the assessments by explaining to them the meaning of the word and how to read the word. A list of common words that are frequently repeated in metacognitive assessments such as those presented in this chapter are provided in Table 6.

Table 6. Common Terms Found in Metacognitive Assessments

After	Guess	Question
Answer	Happens	Reread
Before	Important	Respond
Belief	Knowledge	Retell
Character	Main idea	Section
Confusing	Making sense	Sentence
Describe	Passage	Text
Dictionary	Prediction	Title
During	Preview	Understand
Evaluate	Pronounce	
Experiences	Publication	

Differentiating Surveys and Inventories for Students Who Struggle With Writing

For students who struggle with writing, it may be helpful to replace written responses with visual cues that indicate responses to assessment questions. You can develop picture icons for the repeated responses and permit students to select the icons from a list. Figure 5 illustrates how teachers can create icons to help simplify writing by providing examples of visual responses to assessment questions. The words on this list are common words on the Reading Strategies Awareness Inventory (Miholic, 1994).

Differentiating Surveys and Inventories for Other Content Areas

You can use the sample assessments as models to write your own surveys or inventories. If you are a science teacher, for instance, and you want to find out more about your students' reading processes while reading difficult textbooks, you can easily adapt the questions by adding science-related words to the statements.

Conclusion

The metacognitive assessments in this chapter are valuable resources for teachers who want to understand the thought processes of their students as well as their perceptions about reading. In addition, not only will teachers benefit from the information reported in surveys and inventories, but students also benefit; by helping to develop students' metacognitive awareness and the "why" and "what"

Figure 5. Sample Visual Responses to Assessment Questions

Common Assessment Responses	Visual Cues for Common Responses
Use words around	
Skip	
Ask	
Think	
Relate	
Disregard completely	
Check to see if experiences are similar	

behind the "how" of reading, teachers provide students with increased opportunities for self-regulation. In the next chapter, you will learn how to assess cognitive thought processes using verbal protocol analysis—better known as think-alouds—and the benefits of using these types of metacognitive assessments to create individualized reading instruction.

Books that contain themes about asking and answering questions are valuable resources when experimenting with surveys and inventories. I have learned much about questioning skills from reading *The Art of Fielding Questions With Finesse: A Guide to Handling Difficult People, Sensitive Situations and Tough Questions* by Mary Jane Mapes (1994). I like this book because it makes you think about questions from the perspective of your students.

A picture book that can be read with students to help them understand different ways of looking at things is *When I Was Built* by Jennifer Thermes (2001). The story is told from the perspective of the house, and the house tells its story about the changes that have occurred. This book is also helpful because it can be used to explain before, during, and after concepts. *Choice Words* by Peter Johnston (2004) highlights the importance of teacher language in reading achievement and motivation. Teachers can benefit from reading this book by using the suggestions on how to talk to students when writing survey or inventory assessments. Being aware of "choice words" will help you be more effective at obtaining information about students' metacognitive knowledge.

CHAPTER 5

Think-Alouds as Metacognitive Assessment Tools

CHAPTER GOALS

- Understand the instructional benefits of using think-alouds as metacognitive assessment tools.
- Discover techniques for modeling thinking aloud while reading.
- Learn about effective think-aloud assessment procedures.

The focus of this chapter is on using think-alouds as metacognitive assessment tools. A think-aloud is a metacognitive strategy that enables readers to verbalize their thoughts during reading. This "thinking aloud" can be observed and used by teachers as an assessment method to obtain information about their students' strategic reading processes. Think-alouds are valuable assessment tools for measuring readers' metacognitive ability, and they allow teachers to gather information about cognitive and metacognitive strategies (Pressley & Afflerbach, 1995).

This chapter expands on the student and teacher benefits of using think-alouds as assessment tools and provides guidelines for integrating think-aloud assessments in the classroom. You will learn how to model thinking aloud while reading for students prior to administering think-aloud assessments, and you will discover practical procedures for how to go about administering with individual students.

Rationale for Using Think-Alouds

What is a think-aloud? Think-alouds are respected measures of assessing cognitive ability based on the work of Ericsson and Simon (1984/1993) and are commonly known as verbal reports of cognitive thought. Ericsson and Simon found that the most effective way to get inside the brain and understand thinking processes was to elicit children's thinking through a think-aloud method. A think-aloud is a form of metacognitive thinking because it is a verbal report of what students are thinking about and an explanation of their thoughts as they are processed during reading (Block & Israel, 2004).

One way to have students verbalize their thoughts is concurrently. That is, during the reading of an excerpt of text, students report what they are thinking without any prompting. Concurrent reports are a valuable method if teachers want the most accurate thoughts initiated and verbalized when the student desires to do so. Teachers can also prompt students to think aloud while reading during strategic places within the text. One way to prompt students to think aloud during strategic places while reading is to place a sticky note in the book the student is reading where you would like the student to give a verbal report. Block and Israel (2004) provide teachers with many other ideas on how to guide students through the think-aloud process using visual cues, bookmarks, and flashcards.

Teachers can also invite students to give a retrospective report of their thoughts. A retrospective report is a verbal report given immediately after completion of a task (Ericsson & Simon, 1993). For example, I use the retrospective report with students to have them explain when they used comprehension fix-up strategies. From the retrospective reports, I obtained a deeper understanding as to why students proceed with the task of reading and what they do when they lose comprehension or do not understand something they are reading.

Process-oriented measures like think-alouds can provide valuable information about learners' cognitive and metacognitive strategies, which can lead to more effective instructional interventions that target specific strategies that focus on improvement of reading (Ward & Traweek, 1993, p. 483). Using think-alouds as a metacogntive assessment tool allows teachers to document students' actual thought processes while reading. The verbal reports can be analyzed to confirm or disconfirm which metacognitive strategies are actually being utilized and when. As mentioned in previous chapters, data about students' awareness of strategy utilization and reading behaviors or characteristics should be analyzed using more than one metacognitive assessment, and because think-alouds are the best measures of students' cognitive thought processes, they are valuable assessment tools and can be used with other metacognitive assessments to validate individual students' reading behaviors.

Because the think-aloud methodology can be used as a valid measure of examining cognitive processes, more work using the basic methodology of the think-aloud protocols is supported, but in conjunction with other valid measures as an index of understanding cognitive functions (Paris & Stahl, 2005). Think-aloud assessments are an effective method for obtaining cognitive and metacognitive ability but can be time-consuming to score at first, as it might take some time to become familiar with the terminology or procedures (Block & Pressley, 2002; Israel, 2002; Pressley & Afflerbach, 1995). In addition, teachers should be sensitive to younger children who might have difficulty expressing their thoughts due to limited language acquisition (Clay, 1998; Pressley & Afflerbach, 1995).

Guidelines for Using Think-Alouds as Metacognitive Assessments

When implementing think-aloud methods as assessment tools to gain insight into students' metacognitive abilities, it may be helpful to use the following instructional guidelines in your classroom practice.

Communicate Your Purpose

Prior to using think-alouds with individual students, it is important to clearly define what a think-aloud is for students, and identify your purpose for using this method. Providing an explanation offers students information about the task of verbal reporting and helps them feel comfortable about what they were asked to do during the think-aloud assessments. For example, to explain the concept of think-alouds to students, say something like the following:

> The goal of this lesson is to think aloud while reading text. When you think aloud, the objective is to verbalize as much as possible of what you are thinking. Almost everything you say will be good information. You won't be able to verbalize everything you think, but the idea is to give the best report of your thinking processes that you can by talking aloud. Don't try to plan what you say. What is most important is that you accurately reflect your thoughts or even bits and pieces of your thoughts.

After explaining the think-aloud process to the student being assessed, you may want to give a few examples of what a student might do when thinking, as illustrated in the following vignette:

> For example, you may want to make a prediction about what you are reading, rephrase what you think the text is saying, share an analogy that describes something in the text that you're familiar with, remark on something in the text that is confusing to you, or say anything else that helps you understand the text you're reading. Ideally, you should echo directly out loud what is going through your mind, without paying too much attention to how it comes out.

Demonstrate Sensitivity to Students

Personal characteristics such as age, motivation, anxiety, verbal ability, and willingness to reveal thoughts may influence students' levels of response to the think-aloud (Block & Pressley, 2002; Pressley & Afflerbach, 1995). For example, if a student struggles with communication skills because of a disability, this student would most likely lack the confidence to verbalize his or her thoughts during a think-aloud session. Therefore, it is important to be sensitive to special needs like this student's. In this case you may want to consider using a different type of metacognitive assessment to obtain specific information about the student's reading behaviors, such as an interview.

Use Specific Prompts to Guide Students' Thinking

Using specific prompts with students, particularly younger children, will help to explain reasoning behind answers and to regulate performance (Ward & Traweek, 1993). Some prompts that teachers can say to elicit further thinking from students are as follows:

- Tell me more.
- What are you thinking?
- Can you explain further?
- Can you elaborate on _____?

However, do keep in mind that prompts should help elicit further thinking but not distract from regular thought processes. In addition, teachers who use prompts to elicit further thinking should not add more detail to what the children are saying or elaborate on their thoughts for them. Prompting is most effective if teachers use standard prompts for all students.

Model Thinking Aloud While Reading

Prior to using think-alouds as metacognitive assessments with individual students, it is helpful for teachers to model the think-aloud process with the class, small groups, or individuals so that the teacher can demonstrate for the students the types of thoughts that go through a reader's mind while reading and so that students will have a deeper understanding of how to actually verbalize their thoughts. For example, an excellent piece of literature for modeling think-aloud behaviors is the poem "The Runaway" by Robert Frost (1969). This poem is usually appealing to students of all ages, as the subject matter of horses and caring for animals is interesting to children, and the poem is easy to read and keeps children's attention. By modeling the think-aloud strategy for students using this poem, you allow the reader to discover how his or her thoughts can help with meaning construction while thinking about the text along the way. Begin by reading the poem aloud with the class.

The Runaway

Once when the snow of the year was beginning to fall,
We stopped by a mountain pasture to say, "Whose colt?"
A little Morgan had one forefoot on the wall,
The other curled at his breast. He dipped his head
And snorted at us. And then he had to bolt.
We heard the miniature thunder where he fled,
And we saw him, or thought we saw him, dim and gray,
Like a shadow against the curtain of falling flakes.
"I think the little fellow's afraid of the snow.
He isn't winter-broken. It isn't play
With the little fellow at all. He's running away.
I doubt if even his mother could tell him, 'Sakes,
It's only weather.' He'd think she didn't know!
Where is his mother? He can't be out alone."
And now he comes again with clatter of stone,
And mounts the wall again with whited eyes
And all his tail that isn't hair up straight.
He shudders his coat as if to throw off flies.
"Whoever it is that leaves him out so late,

When other creatures have gone to stall and bin,
Ought to be told to come and take him in."

After you have read the poem, break the poem into sections and tell students what you were thinking about while reading, being careful to model metacognitive reading strategies throughout your think-aloud process. This process is modeled as follows.

Once when the snow of the year was beginning to fall

What is this poem about? What is the purpose for reading this poem?

At first, this poem says "once when the snow was beginning to fall." I guess it probably means it is at the start of the snow. It must be early winter. I am guessing they are in the winter. If I were there, I would be happy it is snowing because I love the snow. I think the fact that it is snowing is important information about how the colt will react.

We stopped by a mountain pasture to say, "Whose colt?"

In this line, I think they are saying "whose colt," because they must be thinking this colt is a runaway, and they found the colt when they stopped by the mountain pasture. This must mean they are in the mountain area so I guess that is helpful information, and it could tell exactly where they are and then I could determine what month it is and determine if it is snowing.

A little Morgan had one forefoot on the wall,
The other curled at his breast. He dipped his head

This doesn't make that much sense, but a Morgan might be a little colt. I wonder what a Morgan looks like? I am not sure about what it means for the colt to dip his head. Maybe he is leaning down, like when you pick up something and you dip your head. I wonder what it means when the author says he curls his breast. Maybe the colt is growling or angry. I am going to keep reading to see if I can learn more.

And snorted at us. And then he had to bolt.
We heard the miniature thunder where he fled,
And we saw him, or thought we saw him, dim and gray,

I think it is funny that the colt snorted at them. I guess I was right when saying he might be mad and growling. The colt had to bolt, and that means running away very fast. I do this when I am running from an animal that might hurt me. Since it says they heard miniature thunder, I guess that means the colt made an awful lot of noise when he was running.

> Like a shadow against the curtain of falling flakes.

The author is using descriptive words to help me understand why the colt is acting the way he is. Dim and gray must be a shadow of the colt after he ran far away, and you can no longer see him. I think the author sees the colt dim and gray because he is a shadow against the snowflakes, and now he can't be seen.

> "I think the little fellow's afraid of the snow.
> He isn't winter-broken. It isn't play
> With the little fellow at all. He's running away.

Now I understand, and the poem makes more sense to me. The colt is not really angry, but he is scared and afraid of the snow. "He isn't winter-broken" means he isn't used to winter or snow and thinks running away will keep him safe, but it keeps on snowing and he is now afraid. I am not afraid of the snow, but that is because I am familiar with winter weather.

> I doubt if even his mother could tell him, 'Sakes,
> It's only weather.' He'd think she didn't know!

Does your mother tell you things that you don't believe? The colt will not believe his mother if she told him not to be afraid of the snow. That is what it means to doubt something or someone. Have you ever doubted anything I have said?

> Where is his mother? He can't be out alone."
> And now he comes again with clatter of stone,

Now the poet is asking about where the mother is. I am wondering that same thing. Why was this colt left out in the snow? If his mother were with him, she might show him how to not be afraid of the snow. The mother could comfort the colt. I wonder why the author asks this question in the poem. The colt is alone, and maybe the author has been alone before and was afraid so he knows how the colt is feeling. A clatter of stone means he is charging at them or running away even faster.

> And mounts the wall again with whited eyes
> And all his tail that isn't hair up straight.

The colt is now climbing up the wall, or maybe the colt is trying to kick down the door to a barn or gate. I think this colt is really scared and maybe even in trouble, too. When have you been scared of something? Why do you think the poet, Robert Frost, thought the colt was afraid?

> He shudders his coat as if to throw off flies.
> "Whoever it is that leaves him out so late,

Shudders means moving really fast, and when the horse shudders, it means he is trying to get the snow off his back and is probably getting really cold from the snow so he shudders to keep himself warmer. Whoever left this colt out in the cold did a silly thing. I guess they are wondering, too, if this animal could be in trouble.

> When other creatures have gone to stall and bin,
> Ought to be told to come and take him in."

When it says that someone should take him in to his place or stall and bin, this means the colt is very disoriented and afraid, and he needs to get to the stable to be safe. This colt needs shelter, and he needs his mother to take care of him. There are many times I feel I need my mother, but I do not want to admit it. This poem could help me understand how to be grateful for my mother and for those people and friends who watch out for me.

Once you have modeled the think-aloud process for students, invite students to read the same poem together in small groups and have students take turns verbalizing their thoughts. It is also recommended that you conduct repeated think-aloud sessions in which you model the think-aloud process with other text types like nonfiction.

Think-Aloud Methods to Use in Your Classroom

Now that you have been introduced to think-alouds and understand how to model thinking aloud with students, you are ready to conduct think-aloud assessments with individual students. At this time, you might be concerned about the time it takes to conduct a think-aloud. The think-aloud methods that follow should take about 15 to 20 minutes depending on individual students' abilities and knowledge level of the think-aloud process. Prior to doing think-alouds with students to collect verbal reports, teachers should be familiar with the procedures and have practiced them prior to working with students.

Recording and Analyzing Think-Aloud Sessions

Before conducting a think-aloud assessment, arrange for a quiet location where students' verbal reports can easily be heard and students are not distracted by the sounds or movements of others. In addition, it is important to decide in advance how you are going to record students' verbal reports. I recommend tape recording the sessions, but you can also write down their thoughts as they verbalize them.

Decide which type of text the student will use and make sure you have it readily available. Will it be a self-selected text? Will it be an excerpt from a basal reader? Will you use multiple text types? Also decide which type of think-aloud you will conduct. Will it be concurrent? Will prompts be used to initiate thinking? Will you also ask students to give a retrospective report after reading?

The following guidelines will provide more concrete steps on how to record and analyze a think-aloud assessment.

Step #1: Conducting the Think-Aloud Task Inquiry.
Prior to beginning a think-aloud assessment, teachers should inquire about the student's level of knowledge about the think-aloud process, as well as his or her comfort level with verbal reporting. The goal of a task inquiry for think-aloud procedures is to make sure students are comfortable with the task of verbal reporting. Questions that can be asked include the following:

- How familiar are you with think-aloud procedures? How familiar are you with the text?
- How comfortable do you feel with the task of verbal reporting?
- Do you enjoy reading?
- What type of books do you enjoy reading?

Asking task-inquiry questions is important to successful think-aloud assessment procedures because if a student is not comfortable with the think-aloud procedures or with the task of verbal reporting, you will need to address this concern prior to having the student perform a think-aloud.

Step #2: Holding an Introductory Training Session.
The purpose of the training session is to introduce the student to the process of thinking aloud. The training session follows the initial interview and occurs when the student is comfortable with the task of verbal reporting. The training session consists of three components. The first component introduces the student to the think-aloud procedures (for an example, see the vignette on page 73).

The second component involves you modeling for the student how one might think aloud while reading. You may use any text or read-aloud as a sample and model for the student what it means to think aloud (see the section on modeling beginning on page 75 for an example of how to model thinking aloud while reading).

The third component consists of having the student practice thinking aloud on his or her own using a sample text excerpt from one of the student's favorite books or the book you read for the modeling of the think-aloud procedures. By using a favorite book of the student's, he or she will have already identified with the contents and characters and will not have to concentrate on comprehension, therefore allowing the student to pay closer attention to how to express thinking while reading. During the training session, student should be given an opportunity to ask questions.

Step #3: Recording the Think-Aloud Assessment Session. To avoid distracting the student while he or she is conducting the think-aloud, it is a good idea to audiotape the session and transcribe the text later. Any interventions by you should also be noted on the recording or during the think-aloud assessment. Use varying types of texts or genres when having a students perform a think-aloud because students may give different types of responses for different text types.

Step #4: Analyzing the Verbal Report. After the think-aloud has been transcribed, you can begin scoring the results. The Think-Aloud Assessment Analysis Form found on page 101 in Appendix A is a template to follow when assessing students' strategic responses. To analyze the verbal reports, make sure you have a copy of the descriptions in front of you. What you are looking for is the level of evidence for specific strategies used before, during, and after reading, and you can use this form to record the number of evident responses. Figure 6 provides a sample of the types of responses students may provide during the think-aloud and how they illustrate specific strategies being utilized.

Think-Aloud Flashcard Assessments as Informal Prompts

You can use flashcards—such as the Think-Aloud Flashcards provided on page 102 in Appendix A—to prompt your students during think-alouds. Students should perform a think-aloud strategy and select the flashcard that goes with the strategy they performed. By reviewing think-aloud strategies using flashcards, students learn to activate these processes on their own (Block & Israel, 2004).

In order to create Think-Aloud Flashcards, provide students with the following items: blank copies of the flashcards, crayons, scissors, envelopes or plastic bags, and a book or text selected by the teacher. First, give students an opportunity to color the flashcards. An alternative to coloring that may be used with older students is using chalk, paints, or glue on three sheets of construction paper. Make sure students have an opportunity to ask questions about the

Figure 6. Sample Think-Aloud Responses Based on Strategy

Strategy	Sample Participant Responses
Overviewing	This looks like a poem written by Robert Frost.
	The title, "The Runaway," reminds me about the time my dog ran away.
Looking for Important Information	There is a horse and it is snowing outside.
	There is something about a shadow so that gives me more information that they are seeing someone.
Relating Important Points in Text	It sounds like the horse is running about because he is afraid of the cold. Therefore, I am thinking that he is outside and not in the barn.
	When the author says the horse was a Morgan, this helps me understand the size of the horse and what he looks like. The author identifies the Morgan as a colt, so this information tells me that he has not seen snow before.
Activating Prior Knowledge	This poem reminds me about the time I was outside in the snow and the snowflakes were falling so fast, I started jumping around in excitement.
	I remember the first time I want to my cousin's farm to ride horses. Some of the horses were outside, but some were in stalls in the barn. I guess the ones inside were not allowed to be outside.
Relating Text Content to Prior Knowledge	This part right here reminds me how people are afraid of different things.
	The author says someone forgot to put the horse in the barn. I remember when I left my cat in the garage, and he was very cold and crying really loud until we let him in the house.
Revising Meaning	I am thinking that the owner might not have left the horse out in the cold on purpose, but the colt escaped.
	I am guessing Morgan is the horse, and it might have injured one forefoot and it has one on the wall. Now the other foot is curled...oh no no no...It looks like he is drinking, and he had his head down.
Revising Prior Knowledge	I think they are saying whose colt...they are...must be thinking a colt runaway and they found it and they stopped by a mountain pasture so it they are in a mountainous area...that is helpful information and it could tell exactly where they are.
	Earlier I thought it was really dark outside and it was night, but it is actually just snowing really hard and you cannot see very well.
Inferring	I guess the other horses are in the barn because I do not see them in the pasture.
	The horse is scared because it is in this new environment.
Determining Word Meaning	I don't know what a Morgan is but I know it is a horse. It must be a very small horse because the author describes the Morgan as a colt.
	When the author is describing how the horses is acting, I am thinking of several words to describe his behavior, like fanatical, or overenthusiastic.
Changing Strategies	I am confused as to why the colt is running so fast. Maybe something is chasing him. I need to reread this again...I guess he was running because he was afraid of the snow.

(continued)

Figure 6. Sample Think-Aloud Responses Based on Strategy (continued)

Strategy	Sample Participant Responses
Evaluating	I enjoyed reading this poem, because I like horses.
	This poem was difficult to read. The words did not help me understand what actually happened to the horse. If owners do not know where their horses are in a storm, then they should not be allowed to have horses.
Reflecting	Now I am thinking about the horse's mother and father. Why weren't they looking for the colt? Why wasn't the owner trying to calm the colt down, so he would not be so afraid?
	The other horses were envying the colt because he was having so much fun in the snow, but the owner would not let the other horses out to join them. This makes me think of when I was sick and I had to sit in my room and watch my friends play in the yard. (Pauses to think) It is kind of strange the colt is scared because you can't get hurt by the snow.
Conversing With the Author	I wonder why the author uses such descriptive words in the poem? Perhaps Robert Frost is trying to tell the reader to just keep animals in the barn during a snow storm, and the animals will be happy?
Anticipating Use of Knowledge	So far I've learned umm...that horses might get scared in the snow and therefore should not go outside.
	This poem will be useful to me when I begin to write my poem about my favorite animals. Instead of just writing about what they look like, I can describe a behavior of that animal.

Areas of Strengths:

Areas for Improvement:

flashcard images and strategies depicted and review before-, during-, and after-reading strategies. Then, cut the flashcards apart on the black lines so that each square is a separate flashcard. Teachers should make one set of large flashcards and laminate them for use with the entire class.

When you begin a book, hold up the flashcards that have the number 1 in the upper left-hand corner. Ask students what they think when they perform each of the pictured strategies. Next, have students perform each think-aloud as they read the first few pages of a book. Have a few readers recount their thoughts in front of the group, holding up the flashcards that represent the thoughts they had. Classmates can also hold up the flashcards of the processes used while a few are reading to the class. Select one of the flashcards and have the students independently perform the thinking process on the flashcard. Repeat this process for the flashcards with the number 2 and 3 on them. When students finish using the flashcards, store them in an envelope or plastic bag so they can be reused at school or home while reading.

While reading a common text, you can perform a think-aloud strategy and ask students to identify it by holding up a flashcard. As an additional activity, divide the class into two teams and award points to the team whose representatives present effective think-alouds that represent the thought processes on the cards you hold up randomly.

CLASSROOM SCENARIO: Boosting Oral Language Confidence

Your students are struggling to verbalize their thoughts when they are reading books orally in small groups. You notice that a few students seem uncomfortable with talking about their thoughts and do not participate. To address this situation in an accessible way, use the think-aloud flashcards to help students who might have anxiety about communicating their thoughts aloud. Use the flashcards with students who work well together. Give them only the flashcards they understand really well and feel confident using. Write down story prompts on the back of each card so that students can just finish the prompt with something they are thinking.

Resources to Enrich Your Understanding

I highly recommend the chapter "A Window Into a Thinking Classroom" by Paige Smith in *Metacognition in Literacy Learning* (Israel, Block, et al., 2005, pp. 261–276). This chapter provides guidance on how to integrate metacognitive instruction with primary students. Along those same lines, another book I recommend to all teachers is *How to Think Like Leonardi da Vinci* (1998) by Michael J. Gelb. This resource helps teachers look at how to teach thinking and cognitive strategies in a creative way.

A picture book that I advise using with students is *Subway Sonata* by Patricia Lakin (2001). What is really powerful about this book is the way the author uses thought bubbles to help the reader understand what the characters in the book are thinking. This is exactly what think-alouds are intended to do: enable students to share their thoughts.

Reproducibles

Metacognitive Principles Assessment Planning Guide

Metacognitive Assessment	Purpose for Using	Expected Outcomes	Works Well With...	Developmentally Appropriate

Teacher Self-Assessment on Beliefs About Metacognitive-Oriented Reading Instruction

Directions: Read the following belief statements. Circle the response that reflects your beliefs about metacognition and reading comprehension.

SD (Strongly Disagree) = 1, Somewhat Disagree = 2, Neutral = 3, Somewhat agree = 4, SA (Strongly Agree) = 5

Belief Statements	SD				SA
1. Metacognition is a cognitive process in which one is aware of his or her own thinking.	1	2	3	4	5
2. A think-aloud is not a metacognitive technique.	1	2	3	4	5
3. Metacognition is a developmental process.	1	2	3	4	5
4. Students who are able to relate textual information to knowledge variables such as self and task demonstrate characteristics of metacognitive knowledge.	1	2	3	4	5
5. Comprehension instruction does not make a difference to student's ability to develop effective strategies.	1	2	3	4	5
6. Learners who have high levels of metacognitive abilities are able to monitor and regulate their learning processes to accomplish learning goals.	1	2	3	4	5
7. Metacognition and comprehension are directly related to reading ability.	1	2	3	4	5
8. Cultural differences do not have an effect on meaning construction.	1	2	3	4	5
9. Different students have different self-regulation mechanisms closely related to their cognitive abilities and this should be taken into consideration by teachers.	1	2	3	4	5
10. Metacognition is a natural process.	1	2	3	4	5
11. Monitoring strategies should not be taught in the primary grades.	1	2	3	4	5
12. Self-assessing does not contribute to the development of expertise in reading.	1	2	3	4	5
13. Students who have developed more effective comprehension skills read more than students who are less skilled with comprehension.	1	2	3	4	5
14. It is easy for students to transfer strategies from one text type to another, therefore it is not necessary to teach fix-up strategies.	1	2	3	4	5
15. Effective readers make fewer revisions than ineffective readers.	1	2	3	4	5
16. When teaching metacognitive strategies to primary students, instruction should focus on teaching new strategies.	1	2	3	4	5
17. Metacognition is an automatic process.	1	2	3	4	5
18. Metacognitive skills should not be taught at an early age.	1	2	3	4	5
19. Fluency plays a significant role in metacognitive awareness.	1	2	3	4	5
20. Teachers should do all they can to help students decode well in order to help students improve comprehension of text.	1	2	3	4	5
21. Planning strategies do not develop metacognition.	1	2	3	4	5
22. Self-regulation of one's comprehension develops with age and ability.	1	2	3	4	5
23. Metacognition can be assessed.	1	2	3	4	5

Personal To-Do List

Priority Level	Tasks	Status
Tasks That I Need to Complete First	1. 2. 3.	
Tasks That I Need to Complete by the End of the Day	1. 2. 3.	

Thinking Backward to Set Goals Maze

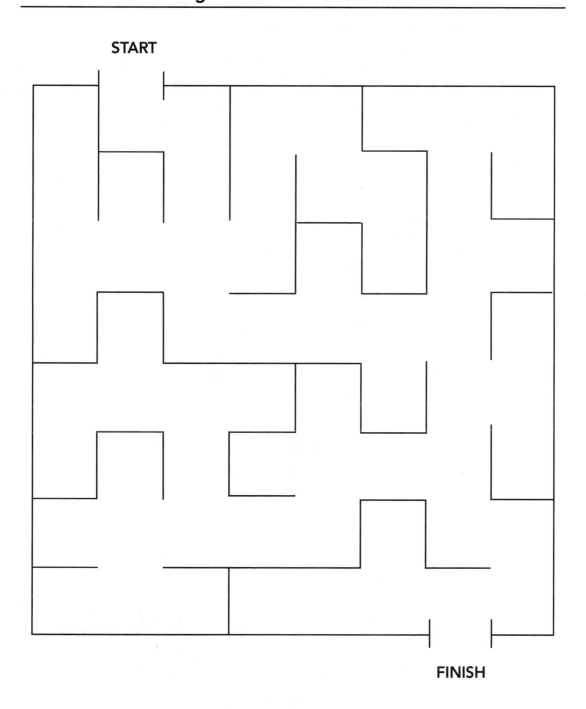

What Am I Thinking?

Instructions: In the light bulb shape, record your thoughts.

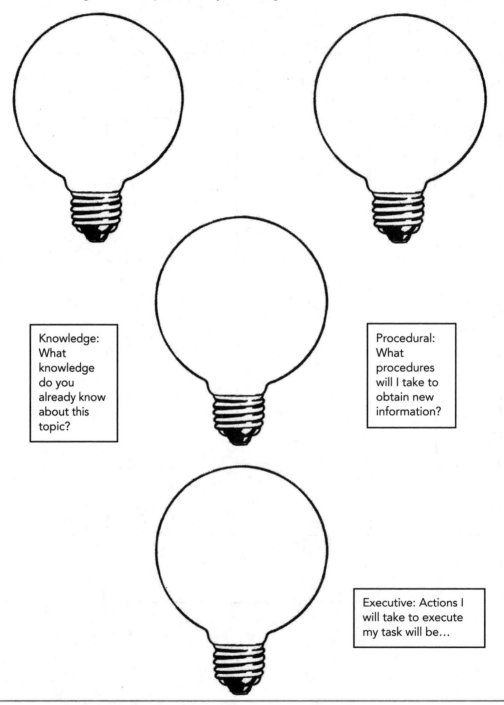

Knowledge: What knowledge do you already know about this topic?

Procedural: What procedures will I take to obtain new information?

Executive: Actions I will take to execute my task will be...

Metacognitive Mind Map for Primary Students

Metacognitive Mind Map for Upper Elementary Students

Gold Ribbon Goals

Goal #1

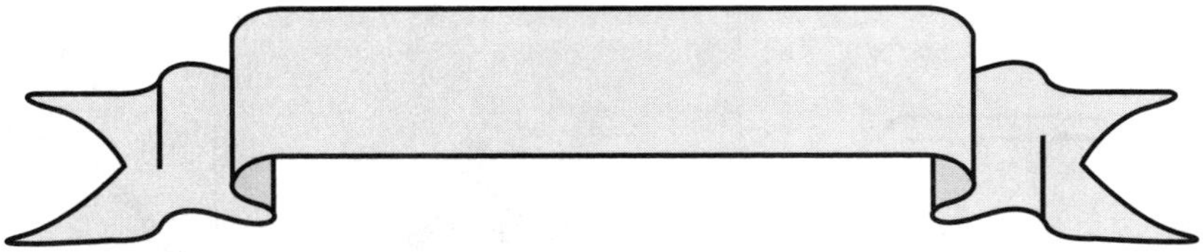

Progress: _____

_____

_____

Goal #2

Progress: _____

_____

_____

Goal #3

Progress: _____

_____

_____

Positive actions I can take to achive my goals:_____

_____

_____

_____

Keeping My Mind on Reading Street Signs

Stop Reading
I do not understand.

Caution
I am getting confused.

Yes!
I understand what
I am reading.

Instructions: Copy figure and have students cut apart at the lines. Explain to them what each sign means and when they are to use the sign.

Metacognitive Sentence-by-Sentence Self-Monitoring Record

Name: _____ Date: _____

Text Selection: _____

Request for Confirmation	Request for Coaching	Cues Used by Teacher	Word or Thoughts Told	Oral Reading Notes
Observations After Coaching	Type of Requests After Coaching	Additional Cues Used	Responses After Coaching	Improvements or Suggestions for Further Improvement

PBI Pyramid

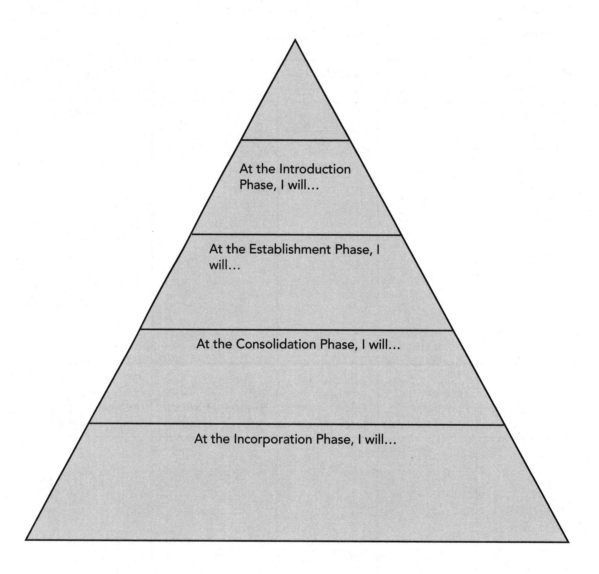

At the Introduction Phase, I will...

At the Establishment Phase, I will...

At the Consolidation Phase, I will...

At the Incorporation Phase, I will...

Back-to-School Interview Form

Student Name: _____ Date of Interview: _____

1. How would you describe yourself as a reader?

2. What do you do before you start reading a book?

3. What do you do when you do not understand the story?

4. When you read a nonfiction book (show sample here), what do you do when you do not understand a word?

5. What would you like me to do this year to help you be a better reader and writer?

Visual Back-to-School Interview Form

Student Name: _____ Date of Interview: _____

This is me as a reader.

This is what I do before I read.

This is what I do when I do not understand a story.

This is what I do when I do not understand a word.

This is what I am thinking when I read or hear a story.

This person is a good reader.

This is what the good reader I know does.

What I value most about how I read is...

Peer Meta-View Prompts

Describe yourself as a reader.

What do you do before you read?

What do you do if you
do not understand a story?

What do you do if you do not
understand a word?

What are you thinking when you read?

Who do you know that is a good reader?

What do good readers do?

What do you value most that
you do as a reader?

Reading Strategy Awareness Inventory Analysis Form

Student: _____   Date: _____

Assessment Question	How a Student Might Respond	What to Suggest to Student for Improvement
1. What do you do if you encounter a word and you don't know what it means?		
2. What do you do if you don't know what an entire sentence means?		
3. If you are reading science or social studies material, what would you do to remember the important information you've read?		
4. Before you start to read, what kind of plans do you make to help you read better?		
5. Why would you go back and read an entire passage over again?		
6. Knowing that you don't understand a particular sentence while reading involves understanding that...		
7. As you read the textbook, which of these do you do?		
8. While you read, which of these are important?		
9. When you come across a part of the text that is confusing, what do you do?		
10. Which sentences are most important in the chapter?		

Using Metacognitive Assessments to Create Individualized Reading Instruction by Susan E. Israel. © 2007 International Reading Association. May be copied for classroom use. Assessment questions from Miholic, V. (1994). An inventory to pique students' metacognitive awareness of reading strategies. *Journal of Reading, 38,* 84–86. Reprinted with permission from the International Reading Association and V. Miholic.

Think-Aloud Assessment Analysis Form

	Strategy	Sample Student Response	Number of Responses
Planning	Overviewing		
	Looking for important information		
	Relating important points in text		
	Activating prior knowledge		
	Relating text content to prior knowledge		
Monitoring	Revising meaning		
	Inferring		
	Determining word meaning		
	Changing strategies		
	Evaluating		
Evaluating	Reflecting		
	Anticipating use of knowledge		

Areas of Strengths:

Areas for Improvement:

Think-Aloud Flashcards

1	1	1
Overview the Text	Look for Important Information	Connect to Author's Big Idea
1	1	2
Activate Relevant Knowledge	Put Myself in the Book	Revise Prior Knowledge and Predict
2	2	2
Recognize an Author's Writing Style	Determine Word Meanings	Ask Questions
3	3	3
Notice Novelty in Text	Put the Book in Your Life	Anticipate the Use: Restating and Reading Ahead

Assessments

Index of Reading Awareness

Score	Items

Evaluation

1. What is the hardest part about reading for you?

1	a. Sounding out the hard words.
2	b. When you don't understand the story.
0	c. Nothing is hard about reading for you.

2. What would help you become a better reader?

1	a. If more people would help you when you read.
0	b. Reading easier books with shorter words.
2	c. Checking to make sure you understand what you read.

3. What is special about the first sentence or two in a story?

1	a. They always begin with "Once upon a time..."
0	b. The first sentences are the most interesting.
2	c. They often tell what the story is about.

4. How are the last sentences of a story special?

1	a. They are exciting, action sentences.
2	b. They tell you what happened.
0	c. They are harder to read.

5. How can you tell which sentences are the most important ones in a story?

2	a. They're the ones that tell the most about the characters and what happens.
1	b. They're the most interesting ones.
0	c. All of them are important.

Planning

1. If you could only read some of the sentences in the story because you were in a hurry, which ones would you read?

0	a. Read the sentences in the middle of the story.
2	b. Read the sentences that tell you most about the story.
1	c. Read the interesting, exciting sentences.

2. When you tell other people about what you read, what do you tell them?

2	a. What happened in the story.
0	b. The number of pages in the book.
1	c. Who the characters are.

(continued)

From Jacobs, J.E., & Paris, S.G. (1987). Children's metacognition about reading: Issues in definition, measurement, and instruction. *Educational Psychologist, 22*(3 & 4), 255–278. Reprinted with permission from Lawrence Erlbaum Associates, Inc., and S.G. Paris.

Index of Reading Awareness (continued)

Score	Items

3. If the teacher told you to read a story to remember the general meaning, what would you do?
2   a. Skim through the story to find the main parts.
1   b. Read all of the story and try to remember everything.
0   c. Read the story and remember all of the words.

4. Before you start to read, what kinds of plans do you make to help you read better?
0   a. You don't make any plans. You just start reading.
1   b. You choose a comfortable place.
2   c. You think about why you are reading.

5. If you had to read very fast and could only read some words, which ones would you try to read?
1   a. Read the new vocabulary words because they are important.
0   b. Read the words that you could pronounce.
2   c. Read the words that tell the most about the story.

Regulation

1. What things do you read faster than others?
1   a. Books that are easy to read.
2   b. When you've read the story before.
0   c. Books that have a lot of pictures.

2. Why do you go back and read things over again?
1   a. Because it is good practice.
2   b. Because you didn't understand it.
0   c. Because you forgot some words.

3. What do you do if you come to a word and you don't know what it means?
2   a. Use the words around it to figure it out.
1   b. Ask someone else.
0   c. Go on to the next word.

4. What do you do if you don't know what a whole sentence means?
1   a. Read it again.
0   b. Sound out all of the words.
2   c. Think about the other sentences in the paragraph.

(continued)

From Jacobs, J.E., & Paris, S.G. (1987). Children's metacognition about reading: Issues in definition, measurement, and instruction. *Educational Psychologist, 22*(3 & 4), 255–278. Reprinted with permission from Lawrence Erlbaum Associates, Inc., and S.G. Paris.

Index of Reading Awareness (continued)

Score   **Items**

5. What parts of the story do you skip as you read?
1   a. The hard words and parts that you don't understand.
2   b. The unimportant parts that don't mean anything for the story.
0   c. You never skip anything.

Conditional Knowledge

1. If you are reading a story for fun, what would you do?
1   a. Look at the pictures to get the meaning.
0   b. Read the story as fast as you can.
2   c. Imagine the story like a movie in your mind.

2. If you are reading for science or social studies, what would you do to remember the information?
2   a. Ask yourself questions about the important ideas.
0   b. Skip the parts you don't understand.
1   c. Concentrate and try hard to remember it.

3. If you are reading for a test, which would help the most?
1   a. Read the story as many times as possible.
2   b. Talk about it with somebody to make sure you understand it.
0   c. Say the sentences over and over.

4. If you are reading a library book to write a book report, which would help you the most?
1   a. Sound out words you don't know.
2   b. Write it down in your own words.
0   c. Skip the parts you don't understand.

5. Which of these is the best way to remember a story?
0   a. Say every word over and over.
1   b. Think about remembering it.
2   c. Write it down in your own words.

From Jacobs, J.E., & Paris, S.G. (1987). Children's metacognition about reading: Issues in definition, measurement, and instruction. *Educational Psychologist, 22*(3 & 4), 255–278. Reprinted with permission from Lawrence Erlbaum Associates, Inc., and S.G. Paris.

Reading Strategy Awareness Inventory

Directions: Under each question, put a check mark beside all the responses you think are effective.

1. What do you do if you encounter a word and you don't know what it means?
   - _____ a. Use the words around it to figure it out.
   - _____ b. Use an outside source, such as a dictionary or expert.
   - _____ c. Temporarily ignore it and wait for clarification.
   - _____ d. Sound it out.

2. What do you do if you don't know what an entire sentence means?
   - _____ a. Read it again.
   - _____ b. Sound out all the difficult words.
   - _____ c. Think about the other sentences in the paragraph.
   - _____ d. Disregard it completely.

3. If you are reading science or social studies material, what would you do to remember the important information you've read?
   - _____ a. Skip parts you don't understand.
   - _____ b. Ask yourself questions about the important ideas.
   - _____ c. Realize you need to remember one point rather than another.
   - _____ d. Relate it to something you already know.

4. Before you start to read, what kind of plans do you make to help you read better?
   - _____ a. No specific plan is needed; just start reading.
   - _____ b. Think about what you know about the subject.
   - _____ c. Think about why you are reading.
   - _____ d. Make sure the reading can be finished in as short a time period as possible.

5. Why would you go back and read an entire passage over again?
   - _____ a. You didn't understand it.
   - _____ b. To clarify a specific or supporting idea.
   - _____ c. It seemed important to remember.
   - _____ d. To underline or summarize for study.

6. Knowing that you don't understand a particular sentence while reading involves understanding that
   - _____ a. the reader may not have developed links or associations for new words or concepts in the sentence.
   - _____ b. the writer may not have conveyed the ideas clearly.
   - _____ c. two sentences may purposely contradict each other.
   - _____ d. finding meaning for the sentence needlessly slows down the reader.

(continued)

From Miholic, V. (1994). An inventory to pique students' metacognitive awareness of reading strategies. *Journal of Reading, 38,* 84–86. Reprinted with permission from the International Reading Association and V. Miholic.

7. As you read a textbook, which of these do you do?

   _____ a. Adjust your pace depending on the difficulty of the material.
   _____ b. Generally, read at a constant, steady pace.
   _____ c. Skip the parts you don't understand.
   _____ d. Continually make predictions about what you are reading.

8. While you read, which of these are important?

   _____ a. Know when you know and when you don't know key ideas.
   _____ b. Know what it is that you know in relation to what is being read.
   _____ c. Know that confusing text is common and usually can be ignored.
   _____ d. Know that different strategies can be used to aid in understanding.

9. When you come across a part of the text that is confusing, what do you do?

   _____ a. Keep on reading until the text is clarified.
   _____ b. Read ahead and then look back if the text is still unclear.
   _____ c. Skip those sections completely; they are usually not important.
   _____ d. Check to see if the ideas expressed are consistent with one another.

10. Which sentences are most important in the chapter?

   _____ a. Almost all of the sentences are important; otherwise, they wouldn't be there.
   _____ b. The sentences that contain the important details or facts.
   _____ c. The sentences that are directly related to the main idea.
   _____ d. The ones that contain the most detail.

From Miholic, V. (1994). An inventory to pique students' metacognitive awareness of reading strategies. *Journal of Reading, 38*, 84–86. Reprinted with permission from the International Reading Association and V. Miholic.

Reading Strategy Awareness Inventory, Open-Ended Format

Directions: After each question, explain the reading behavior that helps you effectively comprehend the text.

1. What do you do if you encounter a word and you don't know what it means?

2. What do you do if you don't know what an entire sentence means?

3. If you are reading science or social studies material, what would you do to remember the important information you've read?

4. Before you start to read, what kind of plans do you make to help you read better?

5. Why would you go back and read an entire passage over again?

6. Knowing that you don't understand a particular sentence while reading involves understanding that...

7. As you read a textbook, what do you do to help you understand what you are reading?

8. While you read, how do you know what text is important?

9. When you come across a part of the text that is confusing, what do you do?

10. Which sentences are most important in the chapter?

Adapted from Miholic, V. (1994). An inventory to pique students' metacognitive awareness of reading strategies. *Journal of Reading, 38,* 84–86. Reprinted with permission from the International Reading Association and V. Miholic.

Metacognitive Awareness of Reading Strategies Inventory (MARSI)

Directions: Listed below are statements about what people do when they read academic or school-related materials such as textbooks or library books. After reading the statements circle the number that applies to you. Please note there are no right or wrong answers.

Scoring Rubric: 1 means "I never or almost never do this," 2 means "I do this only occasionally," 3 means "I sometimes do this (about 50% of the time)," 4 means "I usually do this," and 5 means "I always or almost always do this."

Strategies

Type	Strategy	Scale
G	1. I have a purpose in mind when I read.	1 2 3 4 5
S	2. I take notes while reading to help me understand what I read.	1 2 3 4 5
G	3. I think about what I know to help me understand what I read.	1 2 3 4 5
G	4. I preview the text to see what it's about before reading it.	1 2 3 4 5
S	5. When text becomes difficult, I read to reflect on important information in the text.	1 2 3 4 5
S	6. I summarize what I read to reflect on important information in the text.	1 2 3 4 5
G	7. I think about whether the content of the text fits my reading purpose.	1 2 3 4 5
P	8. I read slowly but carefully to be sure I understand what I'm reading.	1 2 3 4 5
S	9. I discuss what I read with others to check understanding.	1 2 3 4 5
G	10. I skim the text first by noting characteristics like length and organization.	1 2 3 4 5
P	11. I try to get back on track when I lose concentration.	1 2 3 4 5
S	12. I underline or circle information in the text to help me remember it.	1 2 3 4 5
P	13. I adjust my reading speed according to what I'm reading.	1 2 3 4 5
G	14. I decide what to read closely and what to ignore.	1 2 3 4 5
S	15. I use reference materials such as dictionaries to help me understand what I read.	1 2 3 4 5

(continued)

© 2002 by the American Psychological Association. Reprinted with permission. The official citation that should be used in referencing this material is Mokhtari, K., & Reichard, C. (2002). Assessing students' metacognitive awareness of reading strategies. *Journal of Educational Psychology, 94*, 258–259.

Metacognitive Awareness of Reading Strategies Inventory (MARSI) (continued)

Strategies

Type	Strategy	Scale
P	16. When text becomes difficult, I pay closer attention to what I'm reading.	1 2 3 4 5
G	17. I use tables, figures, and pictures in text to increase my understanding.	1 2 3 4 5
P	18. I stop from time to time and think about what I'm reading.	1 2 3 4 5
G	19. I use context clues to help me understand what I'm reading.	1 2 3 4 5
S	20. I paraphrase (restate ideas in my own words) to better understand what I read.	1 2 3 4 5
P	21. I try to picture or visualize information to help remember what I read.	1 2 3 4 5
G	22. I use typographical aids like boldface and italics to identify key information.	1 2 3 4 5
G	23. I critically analyze and evaluate the information presented in the text.	1 2 3 4 5
S	24. I go back and forth in the text to find relationships among ideas in it.	1 2 3 4 5
G	25. I check my understanding when I come across conflicting information.	1 2 3 4 5
G	26. I try to guess what the material is about when I read.	1 2 3 4 5
P	27. When text becomes difficult, I reread to increase my understanding.	1 2 3 4 5
S	28. I ask myself questions I like to have answered in the text.	1 2 3 4 5
G	29. I check to see if my guesses about the text are right or wrong.	1 2 3 4 5
P	30. I try to guess the meaning of unknown words or phrases.	1 2 3 4 5

1. Write your response to each statement.

2. Add up the scores under each column. Place the results on the line under each column.

3. Divide the subscale score by the number of statements in each column to get the average for each subscale.

4. Calculate the average for the whole inventory by adding up the subscale scores and dividing by 30.

5. Compare your results to those shown below.

6. Discuss your results with your teacher or tutor.

(continued)

Metacognitive Awareness of Reading Strategies Inventory (MARSI) (continued)

Metacognitive Awareness of Reading Strategies Inventory Analysis Sheet

Global Reading Strategies (G)	Problem-Solving Strategies (P)	Support Reading Strategies (S)	Overall Reading Strategies
1. _____	8. _____	2. _____	
3. _____	11. _____	5. _____	(G) _____
4. _____	3. _____	6. _____	
7. _____	16. _____	9. _____	(P) _____
10. _____	18. _____	12. _____	
14. _____	21. _____	15. _____	(S) _____
17. _____	27. _____	20. _____	
19. _____	30. _____	24. _____	
22. _____		28. _____	
23. _____			
25. _____			
26. _____			
29. _____			
Total (G) Score _____	Total (P) Score _____	Total (S) Score _____	Overall Score _____
Mean (G) Score _____	Mean (P) Score _____	Mean (S) Score _____	Overall Mean _____

Note. Key to averages: 3.5 or higher = high, 2.5–3.4 = medium, 2.4 or lower = low

Interpreting Your Score

The overall averages indicates how often you use reading strategies when reading academic materials. The average for each subscale of the inventory shows which group of strategies (i.e., global, problem solving, and support strategies) you use most when reading. With this information, you can tell if you score very high or very low in any of these strategy groups. Note, however, that the best possible use of these strategies depends on your reading ability in English, the type of material read, and your purpose for reading it. A low score on any of the subscales or parts of the inventory indicates that there may be some strategies in these parts that you might want to learn about and consider using when reading.

(continued)

Metacognitive Awareness of Reading Strategies Inventory (MARSI) (continued)

Categories of Reading Strategies Measured by the MARSI

Global Reading Strategies (G)	Problem-Solving Strategies (P)	Support Reading Strategies (S)
Setting purpose for reading	Reading slowly and carefully	Taking notes while reading
Activating prior knowledge	Adjusting reading rate	Paraphrasing text information
Checking whether text content fits purpose	Paying close attention to reading	Revisiting previously read information
Predicting what text is about	Pausing to reflect on reading	Asking self questions
Confirming predictions	Rereading	Using reference materials as aids
Previewing text for content	Visualizing information read	
Skimming to note text characteristics	Reading text out loud	Underlining text information
Making decisions in relation to what to read closely	Guessing meaning of unknown words	Discussing reading with others
Using context clues		Writing summaries of reading
Using text structures		
Using textual features to enhance reading comprehension		

Metacomprehension Strategy Index

Directions: Think about what kinds of things you can do to help you understand a story better before, during, and after you read it. Read each of the lists of four statements and decide which one of them would help you the most. There are no right answers. It is just what you think would help the most. Circle the letter of the statement you choose.

Questionnaire Items

In each set of four, choose the one statement that tells a good thing to do to help you understand a story better *before* you read it.

1. *Before* I begin reading, it's a good idea to:
   A. See how many pages are in the story.
   B. Look up all of the big words in the dictionary.
   C. Make some guesses about what I think will happen in the story.
   D. Think about what has happened so far in the story.

2. *Before* I begin reading, it's a good idea to:
   A. Look at the pictures to see what the story is about.
   B. Decide how long it will take me to read the story.
   C. Sound out the words I don't know.
   D. Check to see if the story is making sense.

3. *Before* I begin reading, it's a good idea to:
   A. Ask someone to read the story to me.
   B. Read the title to see what the story is about.
   C. Check to see if most of the words have long or short vowels in them.
   D. Check to see if the pictures are in order and make sense.

4. *Before* I begin reading, it's a good idea to:
   A. Check to see that no pages are missing.
   B. Make a list of the words I'm not sure about.
   C. Use the title and pictures to help me make guesses about what will happen in the story.
   D. Read the last sentence so I will know how the story ends.

5. *Before* I begin reading, it's a good idea to:
   A. Decide on why I am going to read the story.
   B. Use the difficult words to help me make guesses about what will happen in the story.
   C. Reread some parts to see if I can figure out what is happening if things aren't making sense.
   D. Ask for help with the difficult words.

6. *Before* I begin reading, it's a good idea to:
   A. Retell all of the main points that have happened so far.
   B. Ask myself questions that I would like to have answered in the story.
   C. Think about the meanings of the words which have more than one meaning.
   D. Look through the story to find all of the words with three or more syllables.

(continued)

From Schmitt, M.C. (1990). A questionnaire to measure children's awareness of strategic reading processes. *The Reading Teacher, 43,* 454–461. Reprinted with permission from the International Reading Association and M.C. Schmitt.

7. *Before* I begin reading, it's a good idea to:
   A. Check to see if I have read this story before.
   B. Use my questions and guesses as a reason for reading the story.
   C. Make sure I can pronounce all of the words before I start.
   D. Think of a better title for the story.

8. *Before* I begin reading, it's a good idea to:
   A. Think of what I already know about the things I see in the pictures.
   B. See how many pages are in the story.
   C. Choose the best part of the story to read again.
   D. Read the story aloud to someone.

9. *Before* I begin reading, it's a good idea to:
   A. Practice reading the story aloud.
   B. Retell all of the main points to make sure I can remember the story.
   C. Think of what the people in the story might be like.
   D. Decide if I have enough time to read the story.

10. *Before* I begin reading, it's a good idea to:
    A. Check to see if I am understanding the story so far.
    B. Check to see if the words have more than one meaning.
    C. Think about where the story might be taking place.
    D. List all of the important details.

In each set of four, choose the one statement that tells a good thing to do to help you understand a story better *while* you are reading it.

11. *While* I'm reading, it's a good idea to:
    A. Read the story very slowly so that I will not miss any important parts.
    B. Read the title to see what the story is about.
    C. Check to see if the pictures have anything missing.
    D. Check to see if the story is making sense by seeing if I can tell what's happened so far.

12. *While* I'm reading, it's a good idea to:
    A. Stop to retell the main points to see if I am understanding what has happened so far.
    B. Read the story quickly so that I can find out what happened.
    C. Read only the beginning and the end of the story to find out what it is about.
    D. Skip the parts that are too difficult for me.

13. *While* I'm reading, it's a good idea to:
    A. Look all of the big words up in the dictionary.
    B. Put the book away and find another one if things aren't making sense.
    C. Keep thinking about the title and the pictures to help me decide what is going to happen next.
    D. Keep track of how many pages I have left to read.

(continued)

From Schmitt, M.C. (1990). A questionnaire to measure children's awareness of strategic reading processes. *The Reading Teacher, 43,* 454–461. Reprinted with permission from the International Reading Association and M.C. Schmitt.

14. *While* I'm reading, it's a good idea to:
    A. Keep track of how long it is taking me to read the story.
    B. Check to see if I can answer any of the questions I asked before I started reading.
    C. Read the title to see what the story is going to be about.
    D. Add the missing details to the pictures.

15. *While* I'm reading, it's a good idea to:
    A. Have someone read the story aloud to me.
    B. Keep track of how many pages I have read.
    C. List the story's main character.
    D. Check to see if my guesses are right or wrong.

16. *While* I'm reading, it's a good idea to:
    A. Check to see that the characters are real.
    B. Make a lot of guesses about what is going to happen next.
    C. Not look at the pictures because they might confuse me.
    D. Read the story aloud to someone.

17. *While* I'm reading, it's a good idea to:
    A. Try to answer the questions I asked myself.
    B. Try not to confuse what I already know with what I'm reading about.
    C. Read the story silently.
    D. Check to see if I am saying the new vocabulary words correctly.

18. *While* I'm reading, it's a good idea to:
    A. Try to see if my guesses are going to be right or wrong.
    B. Reread to be sure I haven't missed any of the words.
    C. Decide on why I am reading the story.
    D. List what happened first, second, third, and so on.

19. *While* I'm reading, it's a good idea to:
    A. See if I can recognize the new vocabulary words.
    B. Be careful not to skip any parts of the story.
    C. Check to see how many of the words I already know.
    D. Keep thinking of what I already know about the things and ideas in the story to help me decide what is going to happen.

20. *While* I'm reading, it's a good idea to:
    A. Reread some parts or read ahead to see if I can figure out what is happening if things aren't making sense.
    B. Take my time reading so that I can be sure I understand what is happening.
    C. Change the ending so that is makes sense.
    D. Check to see if there are enough pictures to help make the story ideas clear.

(continued)

From Schmitt, M.C. (1990). A questionnaire to measure children's awareness of strategic reading processes. *The Reading Teacher, 43*, 454–461. Reprinted with permission from the International Reading Association and M.C. Schmitt.

Metacomprehension Strategy Index (continued)

In each set of four, choose the one statement that tells a good thing to do to help you understand to story better *after* you have read it.

21. *After* I've read a story it's a good idea to:
    A. Count how many pages I read with no mistakes.
    B. Check to see if there were enough pictures to go with the story to make it interesting.
    C. Check to see if I met my purpose for reading the story.
    D. Underline the causes and effects.

22. *After* I've read a story it's a good idea to:
    A. Underline the main idea.
    B. Retell the main points of the whole story so that I can check to see if I understood it.
    C. Read the story again to be sure I said all of the words right.
    D. Practice reading the story aloud.

23. *After* I've read a story it's a good idea to:
    A. Read the title and look over the story to see what it is about.
    B. Check to see if I skipped any of the vocabulary words.
    C. Think about what made me make good or bad predictions.
    D. Make a guess about what will happen next in the story.

24. *After* I've read a story it's a good idea to:
    A. Look up all of the big words in the dictionary.
    B. Read the best parts aloud.
    C. Have someone read the story aloud to me.
    D. Think about how the story was like things I already knew about before I started reading.

25. *After* I've read a story it's a good idea to:
    A. Think about how I would have acted if I were the main character in the story.
    B. Practice reading the story silently for practice of good reading.
    C. Look over the story title and pictures to see what will happen.
    D. Make a list of the things I understood the most.

From Schmitt, M.C. (1990). A questionnaire to measure children's awareness of strategic reading processes. *The Reading Teacher, 43*, 454–461. Reprinted with permission from the International Reading Association and M.C. Schmitt.

Metacognitive Strategies Inventory

Name: _____ Date: _____

Directions: Complete the following statements based on your thoughts on reading awareness. This information will help me understand how you go about planning, monitoring, and evaluating what you read.

1. What are your strengths related to what you do best prior to reading? (Planning)

2. What do you do to monitor your comprehension during reading? (Monitoring)

3. When you are reading something you are interested in, what do you do to help you maintain comprehension? (Monitoring)

4. When you are reading something you are not interested in, what do you do to help you maintain comprehension? (Monitoring)

5. After you read for a while or when you are finished reading, what happens in your mind with the information read? (Evaluate)

Adapted from Schmitt, M.C. (1990). A questionnaire to measure children's awareness of strategic reading processes. *The Reading Teacher, 43,* 454–461. Reprinted with permission from the International Reading Association and M.C. Schmitt.

Differentiated Analytic Reading Self-Assessment, Adapted for Elementary Grades

😄 = Great   😊 = Good   😧 = Frustrated   ☹ =Need Help

Reading Stage	What Step I Should Do	How I Feel I Do			
Previewing the Text	I read the title, author, and date of publication.	😄	😊	😧	☹
	I scan the text looking for information that stands out.	😄	😊	😧	☹
	I use information to make predictions.	😄	😊	😧	☹
Capturing the Text	While reading, I write down ideas.	😄	😊	😧	☹
	While reading, I write down my questions.	😄	😊	😧	☹
	While reading, I consider the author's ideas.	😄	😊	😧	☹
Rereading the Text	I reread sections of the text that were confusing.	😄	😊	😧	☹
	I reread my questions about the text and sought answers.	😄	😊	😧	☹
Evaluating the Text	I summarize themes and ideas in my own words.	😄	😊	😧	☹
	I think about my feelings about the text.	😄	😊	😧	☹
	I think about ideas and my own experiences.	😄	😊	😧	☹
Responding to the Text	I think how I would use my knowledge of what I read in the future.	😄	😊	😧	☹

Adapted from Afflerbach, P., & Meuwissen, K. (2005). Teaching and learning self-assessment strategies in middle school. In S.E. Israel, C.C. Block, K.L. Bauserman, & K. Kinnucan-Welsch (Eds.), *Metacognition in literacy learning: Theory, assessment, instruction, and professional development* (pp. 141–163). Mahwah, NJ: Erlbaum. Reprinted with permission from Lawrence Erlbaum Associates, Inc., P. Afflerbach, and K. Meuwissen.

REFERENCES

Afflerbach, P. (1996). Engaged assessment of engaged readers. In L. Baker, P. Afflerbach, & D. Reinking (Eds.), *Developing engaged readers in school and home communities* (pp. 191–214). Hillsdale, NJ: Erlbaum.

Afflerbach, P., & Meuwissen, K. (2005). Teaching and learning self-assessment strategies in middle school. In S.E. Israel, C.C. Block, K.L. Bauserman, & K. Kinnucan-Welsch (Eds.), *Metacognition in literacy learning: Theory, assessment, instruction, and professional development* (pp. 141–163). Mahwah, NJ: Erlbaum.

Ashman, A.F., Wright, S.K., & Conway, R.N. (1994). Developing the metacognitive skills: Academically gifted students in mainstream classrooms. *Roeper Review, 16*(3), 198–204.

August, D.L., Flavell, J.H., & Clift, R. (1984). Comparison of comprehension monitoring of skilled and less skilled readers. *Reading Research Quarterly, 20,* 39–53.

Baker, L. (2005). Developmental differences in metacognition: Implications for metacognitively oriented reading instruction. In S.E. Israel, C.C. Block, K.L. Bauserman, & K. Kinnucan-Welsch (Eds.), *Metacognition in literacy learning: Theory, assessment, instruction, and professional development* (pp. 61–82). Mahwah, NJ: Erlbaum.

Baker, L., & Anderson, R.L. (1982). Effects of inconsistent information on text processing: Evidence for comprehension monitoring. *Reading Research Quarterly, 27,* 281–294.

Baker, L., & Brown, A.L. (1984). Metacognitive skills and reading. In P.D. Pearson, R. Barr, M.L. Kamil, & P. Mosenthal (Eds.). *Handbook of reading research* (pp. 353–394). New York: Longman.

Berkowitz, B. (1997). Student self-assessment skills: Focus on success, Part II. *Big6 Newsletter, 1*(2), 4–5.

Block, C.C. (2004). *Teaching comprehension: The comprehension process approach.* Boston: Allyn & Bacon.

Block, C.C., Gambrell, L.B., & Pressley, M. (Eds.). (2002). *Improving comprehension instruction: Rethinking research, theory, and classroom practice.* San Francisco, CA: Jossey-Bass; Newark, DE: International Reading Association.

Block, C.C., & Israel, S.E. (2004). The ABC's of performing highly effective think-alouds. *The Reading Teacher, 58,* 154–167.

Block, C.C., & Israel, S.E. (2005). *Reading first and beyond: The complete guide for teachers and literacy coaches.* Thousand Oaks, CA: Corwin Press.

Block, C.C., & Mangieri, J.N. (2003). *Exemplary literacy teachers: Promoting success for all children in grades k–5.* New York: Guilford.

Block, C.C., & Pressley, M. (Eds.). (2002). *Comprehension instruction: Research-based best practices.* New York: Guilford.

Brookhart, S.M., Andolina, M., Zuza, M., & Furman, R. (2004). Minute math: An action research study of student self-assessment. *Educational Studies in Mathematics, 57*(2), 213–227.

Buettner, E.G. (2002). Sentence by sentence self-monitoring. *The Reading Teacher, 56,* 34–44.

Chapman, C., & King, R.S. (2005). *Differentiated assessment strategies: One tool doesn't fit all.* Thousand Oaks, CA: Corwin Press.

Clay, M.M. (1998). *By different paths to common outcomes*. York, ME: Stenhouse.

Crowley, K., Shrager, J., & Siegler, R.S. (1997). Strategy discovery as a competitive negotiation between metacognitive and associative mechanisms. *Developmental Review, 17*, 462–489.

Dewitz, P., Carr, E.M., & Patberg, J.P. (1987). Effects of inference training on comprehension and comprehension monitoring. *Reading Research Quarterly, 22*, 99–121.

Donndelinger, S.J. (2005). Integrating comprehension and metacognitive reading strategies. In S.E. Israel, C.C. Block, K.L. Bauserman, & K. Kinnucan-Welsch (Eds.), *Metacognition in literacy learning: Theory, assessment, instruction, and professional development* (pp. 241–260). Mahwah, NJ: Erlbaum.

Duffy, G.G. (2003). *Explaining reading: A resource for teaching concepts, skills, and strategies.* New York: Guilford.

Duke, N.K., & Mallette, M.H. (2004). *Literacy research methodologies.* New York: Guilford.

Ericsson, K.A., & Simon, H. (1984/1993). *Protocol analysis: Verbal reports as data.* Cambridge, MA: MIT Press.

Flavell, J. (1979). Metacognition and cognitive monitoring: A new era of cognitive developmental inquiry. *American Psychologist, 34*, 906–911.

Garner, R., & Reis, R. (1981). Monitoring and resolving comprehension obstacles: An investigation of spontaneous text lookbacks among upper-grade good and poor comprehenders. *Reading Research Quarterly, 16*, 569–582.

Garner, R., & Taylor, N. (1982). Monitoring of understanding: An investigation of attentional assistance needs at different grade and reading proficiency levels. *Reading Psychology, 3*, 1–6.

Gill, S.R. (2005). Reading with Amy: Teaching and learning through reading conferences. In S.J. Barrantine & S.M. Stokes (Eds.), *Reading assessment: Principles and practices for elementary teachers* (2nd ed., pp. 180–189). Newark, DE: International Reading Association.

Graham, S., & Harris, K.R. (1999). Assessment and intervention in overcoming writing difficulties: An illustration from the self-regulated strategy development model. *Language, Speech, and Hearing Services in Schools, 30*(3), 255–264.

Griffith, P.L., & Ruan, J. (2005). What is metacognition and what should be its role in literacy instruction? In S.E. Israel, C.C. Block, K.L. Bauserman, & K. Kinnucan-Welsch (Eds.), *Metacognition in literacy learning: Theory, assessment, instruction, and professional development* (pp. 3–18). Mahwah, NJ: Erlbaum.

Guthrie, J., & Wigfield, A. (1997). *Reading engagement: Motivating readers through integrated instruction.* Newark, DE: International Reading Association.

Harris, M. (1997). Self-assessment of language learning in formal settings. *ELT Journal, 51*(1), 12–20.

Harris, T.L., & Hodges, R.E. (1995). *The literacy dictionary: The vocabulary of reading and writing.* Newark, DE: International Reading Association.

Hillyer, J., & Ley, C. (1996). Portfolios and second graders' self-assessments of their development as writers. *Reading Improvement, 33*(3), 148–159.

Israel, S.E. (2002). *Understanding strategy utilization during reading comprehension: Relations between text type and reading levels using verbal protocols.* Unpublished dissertation, Ball State University, Muncie, IN.

Israel, S.E., Bauserman, K.L., & Block, C.C. (2005). Metacognitive assessment strategies. *Thinking Classroom, 6*(2), 21–28.

Israel, S.E., Block, C.C., Bauserman, K.L., & Kinnucan-Welsch, K. (2005). *Metacognition in literacy learning: Theory, assessment, instruction, and professional development.* Mahwah, NJ: Erlbaum.

Jacobs, J.E., & Paris, S.G. (1987). Children's metacognition about reading: Issues in definition, measurement, and instruction. *Educational Psychologist, 22,* 255–278.

Johnston, P.H. (2004). *Choice words: How our language affects children's learning.* Portland, ME: Stenhouse.

Joseph, L. (2005). The role of self-monitoring in literacy learning. In S.E. Israel, C.C. Block, K.L. Bauserman, & K. Kinnucan-Welsch (Eds.), *Metacognition in literacy learning: Theory, assessment, instruction, and professional development* (pp. 199–214). Mahwah, NJ: Erlbaum.

Keene, E.O., & Zimmermann, S. (1997). *Mosaic of thought: Teaching comprehension in a reader's workshop.* Portsmouth, NH: Heinemann.

Kucan, L., & Beck, I.L. (1997). Thinking aloud and reading comprehension research: Inquiry, instruction, and social interaction. *Review of Educational Research, 67,* 271–299.

Laberge, D., & Samuels, S.J. (1974). Toward a theory of automatic information processing in reading. *Cognitive Psychology, 6,* 293–323.

Leslie, L., & Caldwell, J. (2006). *Qualitative reading inventory–4.* Boston: Pearson.

Lowrie, T. (1998). Developing metacognitive thinking in young children: A case study. *Gifted Education International, 13,* 23–27.

Mapes, M.J. (1999). *The art of fielding questions with finesse: A guide to handling difficult people, sensitive situations and tough questions.* Kalamazoo, MI: Mary Jane Mapes & Associates.

Miholic, V. (1994). An inventory to pique students' metacognitive awareness of reading strategies. *Journal of Reading, 38,* 84–86.

Mokhtari, K., & Reichard, C.A. (2002). Assessing students' metacognitive awareness of reading strategies. *Journal of Educational Psychology, 94,* 249–259.

Myers, M., & Paris, S.G. (1978). Children's metacognitive knowledge about reading. *Journal of Educational Psychology, 70,* 680–690.

National Institute of Child Health and Human Development. (2000). *Report of the National Reading Panel. Teaching children to read: Report of the subgroups* (NIH Publication No. 00-4754). Washington, DC: U.S. Government Printing Office.

Palincsar, A.S., & Brown, A.L. (1984). Reciprocal teaching of comprehension-fostering and comprehension-monitoring activities. *Cognition and Instruction, 1,* 117–175.

Palincsar, A.S., & Ransom, K. (1988). From the mystery spot to the thoughtful spot: The instruction of metacognitive strategies. *The Reading Teacher 41,* 784–789.

Paris, A.H., & Paris, S.G. (2003). Assessing narrative comprehension in young children. *Reading Research Quarterly, 38,* 36–76.

Paris, S.G., & Flukes, J. (2005). Assessing children's metacognition about strategic reading. In S.E. Israel, C.C. Block, K.L. Bauserman, & K. Kinnucan-Welsch (Eds.), *Metacognition in literacy learning: Theory, assessment, instruction, and professional development* (pp. 121–139). Mahwah, NJ: Erlbaum.

Paris, S.G., & Stahl, S.A. (2005). *Children's reading comprehension and assessment.* Mahwah, NJ: Erlbaum.

Pressley, M. (2002). Metacognition and self-regulated comprehension. In A. Farstrup & S.J. Samuels (Eds.), *What research has to say about reading instruction* (3rd ed., pp. 291–309). Newark, DE: International Reading Association.

Pressley, M. (2005). Final reflections: Metacognition in literacy learning: Then, now, and in the future. In S.E. Israel, C.C. Block, K.L. Bauserman, & K. Kinnucan-Welsch (Eds.), *Metacognition in literacy learning: Theory, assessment, instruction, and professional development* (pp. 391–411) Mahwah, NJ: Erlbaum.

Pressley, M. (2006a). *Reading instruction that works: The case for balanced teaching* (3rd ed.). New York: Guilford.

Pressley, M. (2006b, April 29). *What the future of research could be.* Paper presented at the Reading Research Conference of the annual convention of the International Reading Association, Chicago, IL.

Pressley, M., & Afflerbach, P. (1995). *Verbal protocols of reading: The nature of constructively responsive reading.* Hillsdale, NJ: Erlbaum.

Pressley, M., Brown, R., El-Dinary, P.B., & Afflerbach, P. (1995). The comprehension instruction that students need: Instruction fostering constructively responsive reading. *Learning Disabilities Research & Practice, 10,* 215–224.

Pressley, M., Dolezal, S.E., Raphael, L.M., Mohan, L., Roehrig, A.D., & Bogner, K. (2003). *Motivating primary-grade students.* New York: Guilford.

Professional Standards and Ethics Committee of the International Reading Association (2003). *Standards for reading professionals—Revised 2003: A reference for the preparation of educators in the United States.* Newark, DE: International Reading Association.

Rathvon, N. (2004). *Early reading assessment: A practitioner's handbook.* New York: Guilford.

Rhodes, L.K., & Shanklin, N.L. (1993). *Windows into literacy: Assessing learners, K–8.* Portsmouth, NH: Heinemann.

Samuels, S.J., Ediger, K.M., Willcutt, J.R., & Palumbo, T.J. (2005). Role of automaticity in metacognition and literacy instruction. In S.E. Israel, C.C. Block, K.L. Bauserman, & K. Kinnucan-Welsch (Eds.), *Metacognition in literacy learning: Theory, assessment, instruction, and professional development* (pp. 41–60). Mahwah, NJ: Erlbaum.

Saporito, B. (2006, January 23). Rebel on the edge. *Time, 167*(4), 46–52.

Schmitt, M.C. (1990). A questionnaire to measure children's awareness of strategic reading processes. *The Reading Teacher, 43,* 454–461.

Schmitt, M.C. (2005). Measuring students' awareness and control of strategic processes. In S.E. Israel, C.C. Block, K.L. Bauserman, & K. Kinnucan-Welsch (Eds.), *Metacognition in literacy learning: Theory, assessment, instruction, and professional development* (pp. 101–119). Mahwah, NJ: Erlbaum.

Schraw, G. (2000). Reader beliefs and meaning construction in narrative text. *Journal of Educational Psychology, 92,* 96–106.

Schunk, D.H. (2000). *Learning theories: An educational perspective* (3rd ed.). Upper Saddle River, NJ: Prentice-Hall.

Smith, P. (2005). A window into a thinking classroom. In S.E. Israel, C.C. Block, K.L. Bauserman, & K. Kinnucan-Welsch (Eds.), *Metacognition in literacy learning: Theory, assessment, instruction, and professional development* (pp. 261–276). Mahwah, NJ: Erlbaum.

Snow, C.E. (2003). Assessment of reading comprehension: Researchers and practitioners helping themselves and each other. In A.P. Sweet & C.E. Snow (Eds.), *Rethinking reading comprehension* (pp. 192–206). New York: Guilford.

Stallings, V., & Tascione, C. (1996). Student self-assessment and self-evaluation. *Mathematics Teacher, 89*(7), 548–554.

Stellwagen, J.B. (1997). Phase two: Using student learning profiles to develop cognitive self-assessment skills. *American Secondary Education, 26*(2), 1–5.

Stow, W. (1997). Concept mapping: A tool for self-assessment? *Primary Science Review, 49*, 12–15.

Sweet, A.P., & Snow, C.E. (2003). *Rethinking reading comprehension*. New York: Guilford.

Ward, L., & Traweek, D. (1993). Application of a metacognitive strategy to assessment, intervention, and consultation: A think-aloud technique. *Journal of School Psychology, 31*, 469–485.

Weih, T.G. (2006). Literature autobiography bags. *The Reading Teacher, 59*, 472–475.

Literature Cited

Curtis, J.L., & Cornell, L. (2002). *I'm gonna like me: Letting off a little self-esteem*. New York: HarperCollins/Joanna Cotler Books.

Donaldson, J. (1999). *The gruffalo*. London: Macmillan.

Finchler, J. (2000). *Testing Miss Malarkey*. Ill. K. O'Malley. New York: Walker & Company.

Frost, R. (1969). The runaway. In E.C. Lanthem (Ed.), *The poetry of Robert Frost* (p. 223). New York: Henry Holt.

Gelb, M.J. (1998). *How to think like Leonardo da Vinci: Seven steps to genius every day*. New York: Dell.

Lakin, P. (2001). *Subway sonata*. Brookfield, CT: Millbrook.

Moulton, M.K. (2006). *Miss Sadie McGee who lived in a tree*. Nashville, TN: Ideals Children's Books.

Perkins, L.R. (2005). *Criss cross*. New York: HarperCollins.

Thermes, J. (2001). *When I was built*. New York: Henry Holt.

Tyson, L.A. (2003). *An interview with Harry the tarantula*. Washington, DC: National Geographic Society.

Zemach, K. (1998). *The character in the book*. New York: HarperCollins.

INDEX

Note. Page numbers followed by *f* or *t* indicate figures or tables, respectively.

A

ACTIVATING PRIOR KNOWLEDGE STRATEGY, 8, 10*t*

ACTIVITIES: additional, 40; classroom, 51, 53*t*; goal-setting, 35–40; for sentence integration, 43

AFFLERBACH, P., xv, 3, 4*t*, 7, 16, 18, 47, 49, 59, 60, 65–66, 71, 73, 74, 119, 121, 124

AMERICAN PSYCHOLOGICAL ASSOCIATION, 110–113

ANDERSON, R.L., 3, 121

ANDOLINA, M., 121

ANTICIPATING USE OF KNOWLEDGE STRATEGY, 10*t*, 82*t*

ASHMAN, A.F., 43, 121

ASSESSMENT(S), 103–119; alignment with instructional goals, 27; back-to-school, 18; communicating goals of, 33; Evaluation of Assessment Utilization in the Classroom chart, 29, 30*f*; goal-setting activities as introduction to, 31–45; Index of Reading Awareness, 50, 54, 104–106; interviews as tools for, 47–55; learner-centered, 49; metacognitive, 15–30, 31–45, 47–55, 57–69, 71–84; Metacognitive Principles Assessment Planning Guide, 86; planning connections, 49–50; of primary students, 61; reinforcement of goals of, 59–60; sharing results of, 60; surveys and inventories as tools for, 57–69; Teacher Self-Assessment on Beliefs About Metacognitive-Oriented Reading Instruction, 87; Think-Aloud Assessment Analysis Form, 80, 101; think-alouds as tools for, 71–84; to use with parents, 18; visual responses to questions, 67, 68*f*

AUGUST, D.L., 121

AUTHORS, CONVERSING WITH, 82*t*

AUTOBIO-BAGS, 52

AUTOMATICITY, 3, 4*t*

AWARENESS: Index of Reading Awareness, 50, 54, 104–106; Metacognitive Awareness of Reading Strategies Inventory (MARSI), 62–65, 110–113; Reading Strategy Awareness Inventory, 61–62, 63*f*, 107–108; Reading Strategy Awareness Inventory, Open-Ended Format, 109; Reading Strategy Awareness Inventory Analysis Form, 62, 100

B

BACK-TO-SCHOOL ASSESSMENTS, 18

BACK-TO-SCHOOL INTERVIEWS: Back-to-School Interview Form, 50–51, 97; individual meta-interviews, 50–52, 52*f*; Visual Back-to-School Interview Form, 51, 98

BAKER, L., ix, 2, 3, 121

BAUSERMAN, K.L., 4*t*, 6, 13, 16, 48, 83, 119, 122, 123

BECK, I.L., 123

BERKOWITZ, B., 121

BLOCK, C.C., 3, 4*t*, 5*t*, 6, 13, 16, 17, 18, 48, 49, 58, 60, 72, 73, 74, 80, 83, 119, 121, 122, 123

BOGNER, K., 124

BOOK BAGS: autobio-bags, 52; favorite, 52

BOOKS, NONFICTION NUANCES, 59

BROOKHART, S.M., 121

BROWN, A.L., 2, 3, 123

BROWN, R., 3, 124

BUETTNER, E.G., 41, 121

C

CALDWELL, J., 123
CARR, E.M., 26, 122
CHAPMAN, C., 29–30, 121
CLASSROOM(S): Evaluation of Assessment Utilization in the Classroom chart, 29, 30f; introducing metacognitive reading strategies in, 10–12; metacognitive interviews to use in, 50–54; metacognitive surveys and inventories to use in, 61–66; think-aloud methods to use in, 78–83; ways to effectively use parent volunteers to create more teacher time, 51, 53t
CLASSROOM ACTIVITIES, 51, 53t
CLASSROOM SCENARIOS: back-to-school assessment decisions, 18; boosting oral language confidence, 83; finding time for metacognitive interviews, 51; finding time to work with individual students, 75; goal setting as strategy, 35; nonfiction nuances, 59; resources, 29; students who lack engagement with text, 8; thinking metacognitively, 48; transferring metacognitive reading strategies across text types, 12; what primary students need to know about assessments, 61
CLAY, M.M., 73, 122
CLIFT, R., 121
COLLAGES, 52
COMMUNICATING ASSESSMENT GOALS, 33
COMMUNICATING YOUR PURPOSE, 73
COMPREHENSION MONITORING, 4t
CONDITIONAL KNOWLEDGE, INDEX OF READING AWARENESS, 105–106
CONFERENCE COLLAGES, 52
CONSCIOUS CONSTRUCTIVE RESPONSES, 4t
CONTENT AREAS, DIFFERENTIATING SURVEYS AND INVENTORIES FOR, 67
CONVERSING WITH AUTHORS, 82t
CONWAY, R.N., 43, 121
CORNELL, L., 45, 125
CRITICAL REFLECTION, ON STUDENT RESPONSES, 60

CROWLEY, K., 36, 122
CUNNINGHAM NAMES TEST, 30t
CURTIS, J.L., 45, 125

D

DETERMINING WORD MEANING STRATEGY, 10t, 81t
DEVELOPMENTAL STAGES, 8–9
DEWITZ, P., 26, 122
DIFFERENTIATED ANALYTIC READING SELF-ASSESSMENT, 65–66
DIFFERENTIATED ANALYTIC READING SELF-ASSESSMENT, ADAPTED FOR ELEMENTARY GRADES, 66, 119
DOLEZAL, S.E., 124
DONALDSON, J., 13, 125
DONNDELINGER, S.J., 122
DUFFY, G.G., 60, 122
DUKE, N.K., 122

E

EDIGER, K.M., 8, 33, 124
EL-DINARY, P.B., 3, 124
ELEMENTARY GRADES: Differentiated Analytic Reading Self-Assessment, Adapted for Elementary Grades, 119. *See also* Primary grades; Upper elementary grades
ELLS. *See* English-language learners
ENGAGEMENT WITH TEXT, 8
ENGLISH-LANGUAGE LEARNERS (ELLS), 38; learner-centered assessments for, 49
ERICSSON, K.A., 71, 72, 122
EVALUATION, 7; Evaluating the Text strategy, 10t; Evaluation of Assessment Utilization in the Classroom chart, 29, 30f; Index of Reading Awareness, 104; by level, 9, 10t; sample student responses, 82t
EXECUTIVE FUNCTION, 5; student behaviors when utilizing, 6, 6t

for, 22, 23, 25, 26–27, 28; key ideas, 21, 23, 24–25, 26, 28; in practice, 16–18; principles of, 19–28, 20*t*; questions to ask before administering, 24; questions to ask when selecting, 25–26; sensitive to reading knowledge and proficiency levels, 20*t*, 23–25; terms found in, 66, 67*t*

METACOGNITIVE AWARENESS OF READING STRATEGIES INVENTORY (MARSI), 62–65, 110–113; Analysis Sheet, 112; categories of reading strategies measured by, 113

METACOGNITIVE INTERVIEWS: for classroom, 50–54; finding time for, 51; rationale for using, 47–48

METACOGNITIVE MIND MAP, 38–39

METACOGNITIVE MIND MAP FOR PRIMARY STUDENTS, 91

METACOGNITIVE MIND MAP FOR UPPER ELEMENTARY STUDENTS, 92

METACOGNITIVE-ORIENTED READING INSTRUCTION, 10–12, 11*f*; beliefs about, 28–29; Teacher Self-Assessment on Beliefs About Metacognitive-Oriented Reading Instruction, 87

METACOGNITIVE PRINCIPLES ASSESSMENT PLANNING GUIDE, 86

METACOGNITIVE READING STRATEGIES, 4*t*; effective at developmental stages, 8–9; introducing, 10–12; by level, 10*t*; modeling, 76–78; transferring across text types, 12; types of, 6–7; utilization of, 6–7

METACOGNITIVE SENTENCE-BY-SENTENCE SELF-MONITORING FOR SMALL GROUPS ACTIVITY, 40, 41–43

METACOGNITIVE SENTENCE-BY-SENTENCE SELF-MONITORING RECORD, 95

METACOGNITIVE STRATEGIES INVENTORY, 118

METACOGNITIVE SURVEYS AND INVENTORIES: for classroom, 61–66; differentiating, 66–67

METACOGNITIVE THINKING, 1–13, 48; additional activities to get students started with, 40; goal setting as precursor to, 32–33; goal setting to enhance, 33; What Am I Thinking? activity, 37–38, 90

METACOMPREHENSION STRATEGY INDEX (MSI), 59–60, 65, 114–117

MEUWISSEN, K., xv, 65–66, 119, 121

MIHOLIC, V., xv, 61, 63*f*, 64, 107–108, 109, 123

MOHAN, L., 124

MOKHTARI, K., xv, 62, 64, 110–113, 123

MONITORING STRATEGIES, 7, 10*t*; Keeping My Mind on Reading activity, 40–41; by level, 9, 10*t*; for reading comprehension, 5–6

MOULTON, M.K., 125

MSI. *See* Metacomprehension Strategy Index

MYERS, M., 2, 123

N

NAMES TEST, 30*t*

NATIONAL INSTITUTE OF CHILD HEALTH AND HUMAN DEVELOPMENT, 123

NO CHILD LEFT BEHIND ACT, 16

NONFICTION NUANCES, 59

O

ORAL LANGUAGE CONFIDENCE, 83

OVERVIEWING, 81*t*

OVERVIEWING INFORMATION IN THE TEXT STRATEGY, 8, 10*t*

P

PALINCSAR, A.S., 2, 3, 27, 123

PALUMBO, T.J., 8, 33, 124

PARENTS: assessments to use with, 18; ways to effectively use volunteers, 51, 53*t*

PARIS, A.H., 3, 124

PARIS, S.G., xv, 2, 3, 16, 17, 20*t*, 30, 48, 49, 54, 60, 73, 104–106, 123

rationale for using, 57–58; resources for, 69

SWEET, A.P., 16, 125

T

TASCIONE, C., 125

TAYLOR, N., 3, 122

TEACHER LANGUAGE, 69

TEACHER SELF-ASSESSMENT ON BELIEFS ABOUT METACOGNITIVE-ORIENTED READING INSTRUCTION, 87

TEACHER-STUDENT CONFERENCES: back-to-school individual meta-interviews, 50–52, 52f; Back-to-School Interview Form, 50–51, 97; conference collages for, 52; Visual Back-to-School Interview Form, 51, 98

TERMINOLOGY: "choice words," 69; language of metacognition, 3–5, 4t–5t; terms found in metacognitive assessments, 66, 67t

TEXT(S): Evaluating the Text strategy, 10t; Overviewing Information in the Text strategy, 8, 10t; relating important points in, 81t; relating text content to prior knowledge, 81t; Relating Text-to-Self strategy, 10t; Relating Text-to-Text strategy, 10t; students who lack engagement with, 8; transferring metacognitive reading strategies across types, 12

THERMES, J., 69, 125

THINK-ALOUD ASSESSMENT ANALYSIS FORM, 80; reproducible, 101

THINK-ALOUD FLASHCARDS, 80–83; reproducibles, 102

THINK-ALOUDS, 5t; analyzing sessions, 78–80; assessment sessions, 80; explaining to students, 73; guidelines for using, 73–78; introductory training sessions for, 79–80; as metacognitive assessment tools, 71–84; methods to use in classroom, 78–83; modeling,

74–78; questions that can be asked about, 79; rationale for using, 71–73; recording and analyzing sessions, 78–80; resources for, 83–84; sample responses, 81t–82t; task inquiry, 79; verbal reports, 80; vignette, 73

THINKING: metacognitive, 1–13, 32–33, 40, 48; prompts to elicit, 74; prompts to guide, 74; What Am I Thinking? activity, 37–38, 90

THINKING BACKWARD TO SET GOALS ACTIVITY, 36–37

THINKING BACKWARD TO SET GOALS MAZE, 89

THINKING LIKE THE AUTHOR STRATEGY, 10t

TIME MANAGEMENT: finding time for metacognitive interviews, 51; finding time to work with individual students, 75; pointers for saving time, 51; ways to effectively use parent volunteers to create more teacher time, 51, 53t

TOURS, INTERVIEW TOURS, 52

TRAINING SESSIONS, 79–80

TRAWEEK, D., 72, 74, 125

TYSON, L.A., 54–55, 125

U

UPPER ELEMENTARY GRADES: classroom applications of metacognitive assessment principles in, 20t; Metacognitive Mind Map for Upper Elementary Students, 92; metacognitive strategies, 9, 10t

V

VISUAL BACK-TO-SCHOOL INTERVIEW FORM, 51; reproducible, 98

VISUAL RESPONSES TO ASSESSMENT QUESTIONS, 67, 68f

VOCABULARY: "choice words," 69; Determining Word Meaning strategy, 10t, 81t; language of metacognition,